Turning up the heat: MI5 after the cold war

Larry O'Hara

PHOENIX PRESS

1994

Turning Up The Heat: MI5 After The Cold War
Larry O'Hara
Phoenix Press
PO 824, London N1 9DL
London 1994

0 948984 29 5

Printed in Britain by Little @

Contents

Introduction

IN JULY 1993, MI5 did something truly extraordinary, and unprecedented in the history of the British secret state. They issued a document entitled *MI5: The Security Service*, which sought to explain and justify their structure and function. This was followed up a year later (12/6/94) by something even more extraordinary (for the UK): the sight of Director General Stella Rimington giving the annual Dimbleby lecture, in which she spoke on the topic of 'Security and Democracy — Is There a Conflict?', the answer being, in her opinion, no.[1] In what follows, I will use both publications (and related official ones) as spring-boards, from which to examine the scope of MI5's activities, as well as 'deconstruct' their ideology. Northern Ireland as such, although unquestionably the most important 'theatre of operations' for MI5, will not be mentioned in as much detail as other aspects of their work. This is because whilst a lot of attention is often paid to Northern Irish matters, other MI5 operations against 'domestic dissidents' do not receive anywhere near as much sustained attention, something I intend to put right, here. That said, there are very few areas of MI5 activity to which there is *not* an Irish dimension, and this will be included where relevant. The recent ceasefire declaration by the IRA, were it to presage a genuine end to hostilities, would cause MI5 acute problems, not least self-justification, and this will be returned to below. Having examined the range of MI5's activities in these areas, I will briefly look at some other concerns, as well as making some observations on the 'state of play' concerning their rivals: MI6 on the one hand, and the police (individual forces, Special Branch and the National Criminal Intelligence Squad) on the other. The opinions of MI5's critics and their immediate prospects, both for survival as well as enhanced powers, will be reviewed, along with a summary of the increasing means of surveillance of daily life available to MI5 and others. Finally, I will attempt to answer criticisms that may be made of the basic thesis of this short book: which is that MI5 is a highly dangerous organisation, not subject to realistic controls. Consequently, MI5 (and Special Branch) need to be resisted to minimise their harmful effects upon the domestic political scene.

Before engaging in 'content analysis' some reflections on the reasons for the two linked events — the publication and Rimington's speech — spring to mind. Firstly, amazement that such displays of apparent *glasnost* have been undertaken by MI5, even if the results are somewhat bland. Secondly, the thought that these 'up front' activities are signs not just of serious expansionist tendencies, but a recognition that without growth the continuing existence of MI5 is in question: hence their drive for a greater public profile. Reactions to the two media 'events' will be analysed later on, but it is noteworthy that (in my view) given the parameters of her ideology, Rimington's lecture was a polished performance, in terms of *style* but her ideological slippages and inconsistencies are of significance, inasmuch as they point to the veritable 'hidden agendae' of the secret state. I must straight away declare my agenda: what most intrigues (and perturbs) me are the hitherto unglamorous and low status facets of MI5 (and Special Branch) — *how their initiatives interfere with and seek to manipulate radical 'domestic' politics.* Thus, that portion of their work will be given more weight than others, when I move beyond the 'theory' to attempting to discern the practice of what MI5 is up to. Whereas treatments of the secret state's activities often concentrate on 'high politics' and international espionage, it is my intention to look at things from 'below'. There has been in recent times a veritable outpouring of books on the secret state, all with some merit, and it is not my intention to replace them, rather to look at things from a different perspective, and introduce new information into the public sphere concerning certain MI5 operations.[2] I am not in the business of suggesting reforms to make MI5 properly 'accountable'; rather I seek to alert activists to the full range of MI5's antics — forewarned is forearmed (speaking metaphorically of course). In the text that follows, for the purpose of clarity, *MI5: The Security Service* will be referred to as 'Brochure', and the Dimbleby Lecture becomes 'Lecture'.

The past — an approved version

In order to assess how trustworthy these documents are, a brief glance at the Brochure's 'historical' section is instructive, if not enlightening. The condensed history of the service on p.26-28 starts off badly, by omitting to mention the 'Zinoviev Letter',[3] then descends into low farce in its statement that allegations of secret state plots to undermine Harold Wilson were met by a "vigorous internal enquiry (which) failed to produce any evidence to substantiate these claims, and Wright himself subsequently admitted that they were false" (p.27-8). This denial (repeated in the Lecture p.13-14) was effectively exposed as a lie by the 'Weasel' column in the *Independent* magazine (24/7/93), and so I will not dwell on it here.[4] Of interest though, is the attempted argument in the Lecture that such a plot couldn't work because MI5 has 2,000 operatives "with a wide range of contacts both in and outside government" (p.14). As if Ms Rimington hadn't earlier informed us that "to carry out its functions, the Security Service clearly has to conduct its operations in secret" (Lecture p.12). Are we meant to believe that the secret service cannot engage in plots because . . . they can't be trusted to keep secrets? Of similar calibre is the Lecture claim that a plot against the government is improbable because it is unlikely that all 2,000 MI5 employees could be "in the grip of what I can really only call 'institutional corruption'" (p.14). Wrong on two counts — first, to carry out a plot or shady operation only a few people *are* needed usually (with others providing a 'support role' whether as patsies or whatever not needing to be aware). Second, to act outside the law against a political group (or politician) deemed a 'legitimate target' by MI5 wouldn't be *seen* as 'institutional corruption', rather as regrettably necessary — this much we know from the testimonies of Wallace and Wright.

Moving from hypothetically to actually sinister activities, the Brochure elliptically reveals that the 1988 Lockerbie bombing was carried out by a Middle Eastern surrogate group on behalf of an un-named state (p.14). In less than a year however, that state has acquired a name; with (unconscious) irony Rimington tells us that MI5 "played a major part in the investigation . . . to the point where the atrocity was laid firmly at the door of Libya" (Lecture p.7). Is this a self-admission that MI5 acted to the full their role in the charade of 'pass the parcel' whereby the evidence implicating Syria was deliberately suppressed by Western governments (due to the need for their Gulf War co-operation), and the 'pariah-state' of Libya was roped in as a desirable replacement fall-guy? Strictly speaking, Rimington doesn't say that MI5 believe Libya to be guilty: just that they are as happy as (almost) everyone else to blame them.[5]

In a flurry of Newspeak that would have made George Orwell shudder, we find MI5 expressing worry that nuclear/biological/chemical weapons technology and expertise possessed abroad "has been obtained from the West, often by foreign agents using illicit methods" (Brochure p.16). This really does indicate we have entered Cloud Cuckooland, when hearings at the Scott inquiry showed much of this 'leakage' occurred with the connivance of the secret state itself! Likewise, the news that MI5 has recently joined the ranks of those "helping to counter the spread of weapons of mass destruction — nuclear biological and chemical" (Lecture p.9) is not something likely to make Western military/arms exporters quiver with fear, for it is not they who are the focus of such 'concern'. Indeed, the whole Scott inquiry was set up as a result of the refusal of small companies to act as 'sacrificial lambs' for the activities of larger companies and the British government itself, engaged in precisely such a 'spread' as a matter of deliberate policy. So, no change likely there.

The absence of verifiable truth about the past is partly accounted for by the ideology of those running the show, or more strictly speaking 'spectacle'. At the start, the Brochure promises that "in order to dispose of some of the more fanciful allegations . . . this booklet provides some facts" (p.4/see Lecture p.3). We are further told that "it is difficult to comment on allegations about the Service without revealing, by what is said or not said, information that might compromise past present and future operations, thereby making its day to day work more difficult" (Brochure p.4/see Lecture p.15). Translated into English: allegations can be refuted by facts which *aren't* facts; the reason being if any *real* facts are disclosed, MI5's work may be harmed. All this is very well if we start with the presumption that they are indeed innocent of any charges that may be laid against them. And if they *are* guilty on any count, then we are being asked to give them *carte blanche* to continue in the same vein. In this case, the rationale for not telling us what devilment MI5 have been up to is that it might prevent them continuing to engage in such . . . This, the unaccountable use of force, is the contradiction at the heart of the liberal state, but no less noteworthy for being so evident here.

New targets and old

Describing the functions of MI5, the Brochure (p.12) tells us that as of July 1993 25% of MI5's resources were devoted to 'Counter Espionage and Counter Proliferation'. This former activity is what might be called 'spying' in the conventional sense of the term, and I have little to say about this, save to remark that uncovering spies seems to be something MI5 has long shown itself to be incompetent at, even disinterested in. The case of Michael Smith, an electronics expert and Soviet spy for over 20 years until his exposure in August 1992, due to a defection rather than any MI5 investigation, is a good illustration of that fact.[6] As for 'Counter Proliferation', while little concrete operationally has emerged about how MI5 is carrying this function out, there are disturbing reports from Germany of secret state *agent provocateur* activity in this area, that I will discuss later. "Safeguarding the economic well-being of the UK" (p.12) is an admitted activity that encompasses all the operational areas to an extent, and is not quantified. As to how exactly this function relates to the activities of multinational companies, or the nascent protectionist bloc of the EC — an area of great sensitivity, at the very least — we are told nothing. The bulk of resources were ostensibly allocated to 'Counter-Terrorism': 44% on 'Irish and other domestic Terrorism', 26% 'International'. A mere 5% was said to be allocated to 'Subversion'. By the time of the Lecture in June 1994, a slight shift was detectable, so slight I have seen no comment on it: 'Subversion' is now allegedly below 5% (p.6), 'Counter-Espionage' below 25% (p.4), with a commensurate increase in the attention given to the Provisional IRA/Loyalists — "nearly half" (p.8). These shifts are minute and may not even be real, that very possibility underscoring the paucity of information available.[7]

Concerning 'Terrorism' specifically, we are told the "Service's principal aim is to pre-empt and disrupt terrorists before attacks can be mounted" by means of the "collection, collation, assessment and effective use of all intelligence on any terrorism affecting the interests of the UK" (Brochure p.13). In June 1994 Rimington gave a potential hostage to fortune by declaring the "threat to British interests from terrorism of international origins is lower than the 1980's" (Lecture p.7). In late July 1994 two bombs went off at Jewish targets in London, as a result of which MI5 was blamed for lack of preparedness: the resulting media fall-out a classic of the *genre* I will return to below. More generally, a point I have made elsewhere is still valid — in a time of budgetary restraint, the best method of keeping on the payroll experts in 'domestic subversion' is to link each group/sphere of activism with 'Terrorism' in general, and 'Ireland' in particular. If this link doesn't exist, it can be manufactured, or projected as a 'possibility', whether feasible or not. *There are some indications this is precisely what has been happening.*

What MI5 are supposed to protect is 'national security'. This is a highly elastic term, which can mean almost anything: Lustgarten & Leigh[2] cite seven uses of it, including one which describes the "range of permitted activities or mandate of a security or intelligence agency" — in other words a cloak which can conceal anything, including a shifting range of targets.[8] This is precisely the way 'national security' is used in the 1989 Security Service Act: something MI5 is charged with the "protection of" (p.1). Such a mission statement presumes 'national security' already exists as an *a priori* state of affairs, which is threatened after the fact. As much as anything else, this perspective ensures MI5 is oriented towards the protection of the existing social order, with all its blemishes, conservative with at least a small c. All that which seeks to promote radical social change is defined as other, alien even. The definition of 'subversion' is nothing new, harking back to the 1985 version which spoke of "actions intended to overthrow or undermine parliamentary democracy by political, industrial or violent means" (Brochure p.12), which therefore encompasses many dissidents of the Left Right and even Green persuasion. Methodological criticisms can be made of the way 'subversive' is used here.[9] Given society is a dynamic entity, what may/may not be defined as 'subversive' is constantly changing, and in order to thoroughly comprehend even official definitions, the society that is supposedly being 'subverted' requires full study in all its aspects, a task for which the secret state is ill-equipped indeed. Also, the notion of *intention* is in this context (as elsewhere) difficult to define.[10] Whatever the semantics, the definition first coined in 1985 was a far broader one than had earlier been used — Norton-Taylor & Hollingsworth cite Lord Denning in 1963, categorising as subversive only someone who "would contemplate the overthrow of government by unlawful means".[11] The current definition portrays as subversive those who think we don't have *enough* democracy, and who may well be non-violent in their approach, even including (logically) the vapid liberals of 'Charter 88'.[12] The 'short-hand' summary definition of subversive offered by Rimington in the Lecture is just as full of conceptual holes as the previous one — she says the "intention to undermine democracy is what 'subversion' means to us. It does not include political dissent" (p.6): yet dissent carried to its logical conclusion could be interpreted in that light (eg anti-roads campaigners who turn to extra-legal action after all else fails). Furthermore, Rimington made a crucial conceptual slip when she first spoke of the role of MI5 in the lecture: its task was defined not as protection of 'democracy', but instead that of "safeguarding the survival and wellbeing of the State against substantial threats which are covertly organised and purposeful" (p.4). There *is* a conflict between democracy and the state, yet for Rimington in this eventuality the state has primacy: expressions of popular will are secondary. This concern for the power of the state above all else is not surprising, but it is gratifying that Rimington allowed the veil of concern for 'democracy' to fall aside, if just for a moment.

9

The collapse of the USSR was a monumental event, none the less so for not being foreseen by the multifarious intelligence agencies. It sent a seismic shock coursing through such bodies, and there was even a refloating of the old proposal that MI5 and MI6 should merge.[13] Such turmoil was understandable given the long-standing secret state premise that all Leftist dissent was 'ultimately' orchestrated from Moscow.[14] The Brochure sees the USSR's demise as having diminished the "threat from subversive organisations" (p.17), this despite the fact that most genuinely 'subversive' organisations have never had any links with, or time for, the USSR. Evidence concerning Soviet funding of official Communist Parties has not compromised groups further to the Left, nor would I have expected it to.[15] The disgraceful antics of the so-called 'Workers Revolutionary Party', which included setting up Iraqi trade union activists for assassination by the regime in return for cash subsidies, is a special case.[16] In the Lecture, there is an interesting development of the argument, which gives an insight into MI5's real thinking. After admitting a lesser threat due to the collapse of Soviet 'Communism' (p.4-6) Rimington lets the mask slip. In a barely-concealed reference to the Socialist Workers Party (SWP), who are by far the major tendency propagating the theory, she admitted the "Trotskyists were fiercely critical of what they dubbed 'state capitalism', but that made no difference to their determination to replace the democratic system with one of their own choosing" (p.6). This is important, because not only does it show all the rubbish about the far Left being run from Moscow was most likely not believed by the bulk of those spreading the smear during the 'Cold War', *the reasons for investigating* Trotskyists and others on the far left have not, on this logic, been diminished by the end of the USSR. For given these outfits were politically independent of the Stalinist regime, and highly critical of such, there is no political (as opposed to emotional/psychological) reason why their capacity to threaten the state should have diminished.[17] So anyone on the Left who feels they are now 'safe' should think again. Whatever opinions I may have about the manifold inadequacies of the political strategy of groups like the SWP,[18] they are *still* subject to state attentions, and perceived as a threat. This is not so much on the grounds of what they do, but what they *promise* to do. For the far left, anarchists, and fundamentalist Greens, whatever their inadequacies, are all in principle committed to constructing an alternative form of society, not just 'minor adjustments' to the existing one. Promise is one thing, an adequate transitional strategy another: at root, the far left are more 'subversive' than they know, even if most members of such groups join and leave without ever having transcended naive apolitical liberalism, the SWP being the classic case in point.

Even before the collapse of the USSR, it was becoming increasingly hard for MI5 to convince ministers of the imminence of socialist revolution, or even major illegality from such quarters. So, in 1990 there were only two phone-tap warrants covering 'subversive organisations', and in 1991 there were none whatsoever.[19] Aside from the unreliability of such statistics as anything more than nominal guides, these figures don't cover those 'subversive' groups (or individuals) that MI5 has managed to 'link', figuratively or otherwise, to 'terrorism': but the statistics do tell us something, nonetheless. This rarity of (admitted) phone-taps around the time of the Stalinist *dénouement* doesn't mean the far left is 'no problem' for the *status quo*. The secret state's anatagonism is highly ideological, irrespective of the current ability (or not) of the far left to mobilise large numbers in the direction of a new society. I certainly take Rimington's expression of continuing hostility far more seriously than I do the ancient caterwaulings of ex-MI5 officer Peter Wright. In a passage that has recently been used (yet again) by far left group Red Action, the far left are written off for being "as dangerous as a pond full of ducks". Red Action "find no fault with that analysis", but I certainly can.[20] In any event, who are we to take more seriously — on the one hand, an operative who even managed to see in Labour PM Harold Wilson a Soviet agent, and in any case retired in January 1976, having spent no time at all in 'F' branch (the domestic subversion part of MI5). Or on the other hand, someone (Stella Rimington) who cut her political teeth in 'F' and 'anti-terrorist' branches, who is now in charge of the organisation? Put like that, there can be little doubt as to whose testimony is more valid *on this general point* concerning current priorities. All the above doesn't mean MI5 necessarily believe the SWP or whoever is likely to overthrow the state: rather they have to proceed as though they think this is *possible*, in order to justify accumulating data, interfering with job prospects, and sending agents into, the far left and other 'subversive' groups.

So, just who, exactly, does MI5 see as the subversives needing to be monitored? Trotskyists and Communists are in the frame for a start, as well as those deemed to be involved in "Irish terrorism", countering which is described as the "services most important task" (Lecture p.8), including both Republicans and Loyalists. The Far Right too get a mention (Lecture p.6/Brochure p.17). The investigation below attempts to demonstrate that the objects of domestic surveillance include, in addition to those groups just mentioned: animal liberationists, Greens, anarchists, and Scottish/Welsh nationalists. Further targets are anyone who can be *connected with* 'terrorism' of any stripe, however speciously. The pointed avowal that there are "no plans for the Service to become involved in the investigation of, for example, the misuse of illegal drugs, or organised crime" (Brochure p.5/Lecture p.9), seems to be another 'economy with the truth', given that as long ago as June 1992 MI5 was reported as doing exactly that.[21]

Before looking in some detail at MI5 actions against target groups, a comment on their admitted scope of operations is in order. The reference to 'subversive groups', attempting "to achieve their goals by exploiting tensions within society" that "by conspiratorial methods . . . have sometimes exerted influence disproportionate to their numbers on *bona fide* professional and trade union organisations and protest movements" (Brochure p.17) is a good approximation of the classical Marxist definition of the ruling class: or indeed MI5 themselves! In a typical piece of humbug, we are told

MI5 looks at 'subversive' "infiltration within, for example, a legitimate protest group. The service does not investigate the protest group as such but the subversive element within it" (Brochure p.18). Aside from the problem of defining 'legitimate protest', this assertion was shown to be meaningless by Cathy Massiter, ex-MI5 operative. She pointed out that because the government wanted CND watched, she was briefed to "monitor Communists and Trotskyists in CND *as a pretext*", and that the NCCL (now Liberty) was also investigated.[22] No doubt with Massiter's revelations in mind, Rimington states "the allegations that the Service investigated organisations which were not in themselves subversive is quite untrue. Our interest was in the subversives, not in the organisations they sought to penetrate" (Lecture p.6).

Just as I earlier took Rimington to be more accurate than Wright, here, inasmuch as there is a conflict, I take Massiter to be more accurate than Rimington. The difference between Wright and Massiter is that she (unlike him) was speaking of matters that directly concerned her work, so much so that she resigned over them. Rimington has a transparent motive for lying, given at the time (1984-5) she was heavily involved in attempts to break the miner's strike, as will hopefully be illustrated by the much-delayed book from Seamas Milne *The Enemy Within*. At the time of writing, this book has been delayed, I understand due to 'legal reasons', for a year or so. If the revelations in it are as politically explosive as promised by pre-publicity, it is easy to see why it should have been suppressed. The problem that will have been faced by Milne is that no MI5 operative (present or past) is likely to want to 'go on the record' with disclosures of murky dealings for fear of being imprisoned, which can now occur for doing such, as will be seen in Chapter 2. Returning to Massiter vs Rimington, there is a clear reason for Rimington to disseminate falsehoods here — none has been advanced for Massiter.

This is not to say that Massiter's utterances should be seen as the last word on either the targets or extent of MI5 'dirty tricks'. One Leftist commentator has suggested to me quite forcefully that those the '20:20' programme admitted MI5 used/targetted were either safely dead (Harry Newton), politically harmless (Harriet Harman), or people the state wanted to embarrass by casting doubt on their judgement (veteran anti-nuclear activist Pat Arrowsmith). On this reading, past operations/agents were gone into to an extent, but (NCCL apart) at the expense of contemporary ones: such as the miner's strike, which Massiter personally wouldn't have been expected to know much about anyway, given her resignation was in February 1984. One motive behind the programme might have been the desire to 'bounce' Thatcher into broadening the definition of MI5's 'legitimate targets', else she (and the government as a whole) would look foolish indeed. Certainly, just after Massiter's resignation, as a result of the Bettaney spy case,[23] Thatcher set up in March 1984, a broad-ranging Inquiry into MI5. They would have been worried about this, the potential danger caused by Massiter's full revelations, and the recent acquittal by a jury of senior civil servant Clive Ponting, for leaking official secrets concerning the Falklands War, especially as he had used the defence of 'public interest' (later abolished). In this respect, it would have been a master-stroke of damage-limitation by MI5 to have allowed reference to instructions given by Tory politicians to focus heavily on CND in 1982. A right-wing Tory government would feel bound to defend such actions, and in legitimating them would also be sanctioning the broad range of targets that *MI5 had already been surveilling anyway*. '20:20 Vision' could be seen as a highly effective damage limitation exercise, whereby MI5 'got in first' before their critics, assuaging Labour fears of their good faith.[24] This is only a hypothesis of course, but US experience of Iran-Contra shows that one highly effective means of limiting political damage is to release dated and or diversionary morsels, so as to steer researchers in all the wrong directions. Revelations about the NCCL being targetted were no doubt shocking to Harman and Hewitt, but hardly constituted news, the NCCL having been known to be a target as far back as the 1930's.[25] From an MI5 viewpoint, with an eye to a possible future change of government, a discreet approach to the Labour Party leadership, in which Tory 'politicisation' of their work (an undeniable fact[26] was complained about, coupled with a promise to 'come clean' in the public domain (ie Massiter's revelations, especially about Hewitt who was Kinnock's Press Secretary), and an expressed desire to be placed on a statutory footing (not to come till 1989), would be a smart move. It would certainly take the wind out of the sails of any putative Labour attempt to reform the intelligence services, something that had been mooted in 1983. Just a thought. The suggestion here isn't that Massiter was lying, but simply that she wasn't disclosing the whole truth, perhaps in return for a promise of immunity from prosecution? This doesn't question her individual motives, but might explain the limits to her revelations, and those of the programme. Another explanation for the limited disclosure might be that she may not have known more outside her personal remit: while MI5 gets up to all sorts of nefarious activities, it doesn't necessarily follow that officers will discuss such even with their close colleagues.[27]

Returning to the present, the dominant *leitmotif* recurring throughout MI5's self-justification is that of terrorism and the need to counter it. With this in mind, any group deemed to be of interest can find itself, if shown to be putatively, actively or even hypothetically linked to 'terrorism', reclassified and upgraded by administrative *fiat*. The windows of opportunity for this to happen (aside from sheer invention) are potentially provided by police failings. Lustgarten & Leigh describe a "form of tautology: a number of incidents occur; there are political overtones; the police are unable to catch the offenders; *ergo* this must amount to activity so 'organized' that it rises to a threat to national security. On this reasoning, so would Robin Hood and his merry men".[28] This doesn't happen in all cases: but it is MI5 who take the decision initially, however much they may sometimes seek to offload the blame onto their nominal political masters. It is the process of target classification and reclassification that expends much intellectual energy, and in its fluidity and dynamism is most absorbing, from a subject point of view. It is also crucial to MI5's rampant unaccountability.

MI5's methods — their own account

The methods MI5 admits to employing are those we might expect — public record scanning, eavesdropping, interception of communications, surveillance and running agents (Brochure p.20-1/Lecture p.10). The central illusion here is the declaration that MI5 is constrained by the 1989 Security Service Act, which placed them on a statutory footing for the first time. According to current Home Secretary Michael Howard, the "Act is fundamental to all aspects of the work of the Service, and therefore lies at the heart of government policy" (Brochure p.3). That may well (arguably) reflect *his* belief, and what the government *thinks* is happening, but as neither he nor the PM is in a position to gather independent information, there is no guarantee they necessarily know what is going on. For her part, Rimington is quite happy to put on record the fact that "members of the Service at all levels regard the legal framework which the Security Service Act provides as fundamental to everything we do — and we welcomed it warmly" (Lecture p.12). That such fulsome praise is heaped on such a document rings alarm bells straight away, a suspicion only increased by viewing the Act.[29] Its very brevity (7.5 pages) indicates there is little mileage to be got from this text. This is hardly surprising, for, as Gill has pointed out, the Act was not introduced to bring about any real 'accountability' but to minimise criticism in the wake of the 1987 Spycatcher case and the legal forays of Harman/Hewitt against MI5.[30] The Act contains passages of undeniable interest, most notably the reference to an MI5 function of "preventing or detecting serious crime" that has been forgotten by some observers (and operatives!), and might go some way to explaining their tussle with the police-controlled National Criminal Intelligence Service (NCIS). Interference with property or premises is not to be allowed unless it can lead to "obtaining information which . . . is likely to be of substantial value in assisting the Service to discharge any of its functions: and cannot reasonably be obtained by other means (p.2). In other words, targets are not likely to be burgled . . . unless MI5 decides it is necessary! The Intelligence Services Bill of 1993 extends the possibility of interference by MI5 (and MI6/GCHQ) even further: not just the gathering of information but anything that might assist in the exercise of "statutory functions". This means that planting forged documents or even (in principle) explosives on the premises of suspects would be legitimated (Clause 5:2a). The model of activity MI5 would have us believe they adhere to is very much an extension of what we might call the standard 'police' model: they observe, investigate monitor and then report. This connotes a passive stance in relation to the objects of their attention, something which the above interventionist aspects of their remit contradict. I will further contend below that MI5's operations, far from conforming to the 'police' model are highly participative, even instigatory.

Reading the runes

So much for the theory of what MI5 is supposedly up to; what about the practice? Straight away it must be acknowledged that most of their activity is shrouded in mystery. For example, of the c.2,000 direct employees MI5 owns up to having, only 340 are said to be in the 'General Intelligence Group', "responsible for much of the Service's investigation, assessment and policy work, as well as operational tasks", including "the recruitment of agents" (Brochure p.9). Thus, there is no proper answer here to the wholly justifiable question — just how many infiltrators/agents are there inside the radical political groups defined as 'subversive'? Massiter's answer (in 1985) was "hundreds". An indication of the budgetary pressures MI5 are facing has been provided by recent information, putting current establishment numbers at 2,235 in 1994, with a planned reduction to 2,189 in 1995.[31] The second limitation on analysing what MI5 are up to is the necessary reliance of those outside their 'charmed circle' of media flunkeys on what is filtered through that prism. The role of the media in uncritically recycling secret state propaganda, accepting their terminology, and willingly engaging in campaigns to set up and target individuals/groups, is one of the least remarked upon but most unpleasant features of our time.[32] By definition, when it comes to making sense of MI5's activities, disentangling fact from fiction from disinformation is a hazardous and delicate enterprise. Thus, initially, we have four things to go on: official documents and the testimony of former officers/agents; close textual and conjunctural analysis of disinformation campaigns; what is disclosed in/surrounding various court cases; and detailed observation of various milieux. Without this last source of knowledge, an understanding of events 'on/under the ground', analysis would be reduced to the routine level of the tame media — confined and self-referential pap. Happily, the internecine conflicts between Special Branch and MI5 have hardly ceased since the latter formally wrested control of 'mainland' anti-IRA operations from the former in May 1992, so succulent morsels of information detrimental to MI5 surface from time to time in the media still. A striking example of this was the *Sunday Times* publishing clues about Stella Rimington's home address/financial transactions (7/3/93).[33]

Given MI5 have long been agitating for unrestricted access to the Police National Computer (and now seem to have got it), the declaration that nobody else is allowed access to *their* computer network could be seen as another shot in the ongoing battle between MI5 and the police (Brochure p.22). Not content with control over 'mainland' anti-IRA intelligence, "there is a growing suspicion among Special Branch officers that MI5 intends taking the lead in Northern Ireland" (on which more below).[34] It may well have been RUC Special Branch annoyance at this prospect that led them to provide Keith Dovkants with the highly detailed information used in his excellent article for the (London) *Evening Standard* on MI5's November 1993 'sting' concerning sales of Polish arms to Ulster Loyalists, on which more below.[35]

It was this piece that triggered the imposition of a 'D' notice, but also alerted those outside the UK not subject to such restrictions (such as the Southern Irish press and Paris-based *Intelligence Newsletter*), that there was a good story. This episode didn't enter the public domain by chance: Dovkant's article highly embarrassed MI5, all the more so for being printed in the daily paper of England's capital, close to the nerve-centres of power. A final source of data about MI5 — especially now when they are seeking to expand their powers and range of targets — is the incidental legislation necessary to legitimate parts of that expansion, including parts of the Criminal Justice Bill, as well as other ideas insistently floated by their minions.

Notes:

1   This lecture was subsequently published verbatim by the BBC Education Department in July 1994, and all quotations are from this publication.

2   The classic work on the malign influence of the secret state is Stephen Dorril & Robin Ramsay's 'Smear!: Wilson & the Secret State' (Fourth Estate 1991), to which all who desire to take the secret state seriously must acknowledge their debt. In particular, as well as the close attention to detail and careful analysis, axiomatic to this book (and reality itself) is the concept of 'inter-agency rivalry' which is a great help to those of us on the 'outside' in making sense of events. For a highly-detailed and informative orthodox view of some current developments, which is critical to an extent even if somewhat anodyne, see Stephen Dorril 'The Silent Conspiracy' (Heinemann London 1993). Another useful overview of theoretical/practical issues is Peter Gill 'Policing Politics' (Frank Cass London 1994). Finally here, mention must be made of Laurence Lustgarten and Ian Leigh 'In From The Cold' (Oxford University Press 1994). This book consciously avoids concentration on analysing specific operations, but makes up for this by highly-detailed analysis of court cases, ideological concepts, and the informative glimpses of higher-level 'operational ideology' that the authors were afforded as a result of extensive interviews with 'insiders']

3   A spurious letter, supposedly written by the Chair of the (USSR-controlled) Communist International (COMINTERN) to the British Communist Party, giving them instructions as to how to work with the Labour Party in organising an armed insurrection. The leakage of this document, most probably a secret state forgery, was thought to have contributed to the electoral defeat of the first minority Labour government in 1924 — as it was intended to.

4   Peter Wright was a former MI5 scientific officer who on his own admission was involved in plots to destabilise the Wilson government in 1974. This was outlined in his book *Spycatcher* (Heinemann 1987), which the government unsuccessfully attempted to suppress. The publicity given to Wright conveniently ignored the fact that the first detailed analysis of attempts at subverting the Wilson government were contained in the earlier issue 11 of *Lobster* (1986), partly based on Colin Wallace's information.

5   For a detailed examination of the likely complicity of Syria, and the Western cover-up,

see Donald Goddard & Lester Coleman *Trail of the Octopus — From Beirut to Lockerbie* (Penguin 1994)]

6   See the articles summarising the case by David Connett/James Cusick (*Independent* 19/11/93) and Lawrence Donegan/Richard Norton-Taylor (*Guardian* 19/11/93). Smith received a 25 year jail sentence: had he gone to Oxbridge he'd no doubt have received a knighthood.

7   The change may be illusory because the Lecture doesn't use exact numbers except for the term 'Subversion' and even there the 1993 Brochure figure may have been rounded up. Also, the Lecture doesn't specify the exact proportion of resources now (supposedly) earmarked to 'Counter-Proliferation' separately, and so on.

8   *Op. cit.* p.322-23]

9   For detailed scrutiny of the concept of 'subversion' as applied in the UK see Lustgarten & Leigh *op. cit.* p.395-405.

10 Some of these points have been made by Patrick Harrington in the (unattributed) article 'When The State Becomes Subversive' (*Nationalism Today* 45 April 1989 p.12-13). Harrington's own relationship to the state is a subject I will return to, elsewhere.

11 *Blacklist* Hogarth 1988 p.5.

12 Norton Taylor & Hollingsworth argue (*op. cit.* p.8) that one reason for Thatcher's wider definition in 1985 was the desire to retrospectively legitimise wide-ranging MI5 surveillance activities disclosed the previous month by disillusioned former operative Cathy Massiter. 'Let Practice Find Its Theory' as the Situationists say . . .

13 See the *Guardian* 13/3/90.

14 For an example of this mentality run riot see Brian Crozier *Free Agent* (Harper & Collins 1993). When, at a Libertarian Alliance conference on the Security Services in November 1993, I put to him the point that both the Western and former Soviet intelligence agencies were (are) the key threat to their *own* peoples, he was, literally, unable to answer!!.

15 See the recent summary of known data, plus some conjecture, by Robin Ramsay in 'Moscow Gold', *Lobster* 25, June 1993 p.3-6, which reaches the startling conclusion that "after 1958" (when the Moscow Gold route was discovered) "the 'Communist threat' in Britain was chiefly coming courtesy not of Moscow, but of MI5" (p.5).

16 See *Solidarity* Spring 1986 issue 11, articles by Robin Blick 'The 57th Variety Act' and Ken Weller 'The Party's Over'. They report that *Newsline* photographers delivered pictures of Iraqi Communist Party members to the Iraqi Embassy, and when a motion came before the WRP Central Committee to approve the execution in March 1979 of Iraqi dissidents, including one (Talib Suwailh) who had been a 'fraternal delegate' to a WRP front organisation five months earlier, only *one* member dissented. This indicates that while there were (and are, in my personal experience) persons of integrity in the WRP, the political cancer eating away at the organisation involved *all* factions. On the sordid affair of WRP funding from Iraq Libya and elsewhere see also 'The Revolution Betrayed' in *Solidarity* Spring 1988 p.3-10.

17 This thesis directly contradicts the idiotic and politically illiterate piece by one Sarah Baxter in the *Sunday Times* (19/6/94), who retrospectively identifies socialism with cheerleading for various regimes around the world, and after having (allegedly) listened to Rimington's lecture still expressed a desire to hear "MI5's new definition of subversive". With this

quality of intellect and recall, Baxter wouldn't even be any good as a circulator of disinformation! I seem to remember Baxter was at one time in the Communist Party, and if so, this would be yet another example of that distasteful tendency whereby Stalinists, having for decades traduced socialism by identifying it with attachment to sundry foreign regimes, now feel the need to retrospectively (and dishonestly) implicate non-Stalinists too. If truth be told, the difference between acting as contemptible apologists for Stalinist regimes and nowadays seeking to shore up capitalism is but a small step: the career of Martin Jacques being only the most vivid example.

18 On which see the wickedly hilarious (and all too accurate) *Carry on recruiting* by Trotwatch, AK Press October 1993.

19 See the 1991 and 1992 reports of the Commissioner overseeing the 'Interception of Communications Act' (1985): a topic covered in Chapter 2.

20 *Red Action* 68 Summer 1994 p.1.

21 See the *Guardian* 26/6/92, and also the *Independent* 25/1/93, this last article written by the ubiquitous Ken Hyder, of whom more below.

22 *Observer* 10/3/85 (my emphasis).

23 He was an MI5 officer who defected on ideological grounds to the KGB: sincerely believing that he was advancing the cause of Marxist revolution by so doing. He received a 23 year jail sentence, and although many of his concerns about MI5 targetting of dissidents were similar to Massiter's, censorship of the trial prevented much of this coming out. He was (and as far as I know is) imprisoned under a regime of strict surveillance, and as late as 1991 was still seen as a 'security risk', admittedly by that noted fantasist and disinformer ex-KGB agent Oleg Gordievsky (see the *Guardian* 5/11/91.

24 Such a view can only be reinforced by the fact that the sole researcher credited on the programme was Gerry Gable, *Searchlight* editor and unquestionable MI5 asset. His involvement cannot possibly be explained on grounds of competence: he has never exhibited any profound knowledge of the secret state, before or since, other than to retail their propaganda, and smear groups MI5 was (is) interested in. In 1985 for example, this included the anarchists organising 'Stop The City' events in London, one element of which, Class War, was depicted as fascist, using information derived (proximately) from him. The producers having him as a researcher would definitely ensure that MI5's ultimate interests wouldn't be harmed, and could be seen as a clear token of 'good faith' in terms of self-limitation.

25 See Tony Bunyan *The Political Police in Britain* (Quartet 1977) p.121, and also p.209 on the 1960's.

26 See Dorril *op. cit.* p.17-35 for numerous examples, excluding however, *any reference at all* other than one and a half lines, to MI5 and the 1984-5 Miner's Strike. How very odd...

27 Even aside from 'sub-contracted' operations like, say, the murder of Hilda Murrell.

28 *Op. cit.* p.383 If Robin Hood *did* exist, then this categorisation of him would undoubtedly be correct: although there is a small possibility that declared allegiance to Richard the Lionheart, and Robin's nobility, might mark his merry men down as the first 'pseudo-gang' (using Kitson's terminology).

29 ISBN 0 10 540589 2 (HMSO) 1989.

30 On the Act, see more below. Gill *op. cit.* p.290-6 covers the 1989 Act.

31 *Statewatch* March-April 1994 p.12 reports this, having gleaned the information from Treasury supply estimates. 1994 and planned 1995 figures for MI6 are 2,303/2,251, and GCHQ 6,228/6,076.

32 As I have found in my efforts to bring to wider attention the shady activities of the MI5-linked *Searchlight* magazine, the last thing media types are interested in is investigating the secret state connections of their colleagues. A rare exception was the research of David Leigh and Paul Lashmar in the late 1980's, as evidenced for instance in their exposing MI5 attempts to manipulate the media and directly hire personnel. On this see the *Observer* 4/10/87, which reported a recruiting drive had started in 1976, during the course of which ITN journalist Jon Snow was offered — and refused — secret monthly tax-free payments in return for spying on his Left-wing colleagues. Leigh and Lashmar's sterling work publicising the employment blacklisting activities of the 'Economic League' also deserves a mention (*Observer* 4/9/88), although in this latter case I can't help feeling that the Economic League had outlived its usefulness to the bulk of the capitalist class, and was therefore a 'soft target' ripe for being picked off. Another positive aspect to Leigh's career, although more controversial in the sense that it sought to imply that Peter Wright was far more isolated than he actually was, is his book on *The Wilson Plot* (Heinemann 1988). I mention these early good things about Leigh's career because they have not, to my knowledge, been sustained. The vast majority of journalists don't *start out* as state assets — they mutate into such for a variety of reasons. Partly, it's common sense: as David Leigh will have found, no doubt, continuing to expose secret state manipulation of the media isn't the ideal way to get on. That David Leigh is now associated with the *World In Action* documentary team (on the basis of recent programmes) means exposure of secret state media hirelings isn't an activity he'll be returning to in a hurry . . . In the text that follows, I will not refrain from naming journalists where I think it relevant, and you, the readers, will have to make up your own minds as to whether they are playing a key participative part in secret state disinformation campaigns, or merely reporting such. Some journalists have no qualms about discussing state links: James Adams speaks of "covert relationships" with journalists that "allowed MI5 considerable secret influence" (*op. cit.* p.98). Others are more vague, for instance Dorril has a chapter on 'Honourable Correspondents' which promises more than it delivers: alleging many Foreign Correspondents work for MI6, but only naming a few assets such as Adams himself (who is so blatant, frankly, he might as well walk around with an MOD number tattooed on his forehead) and the late unlamented Robert Maxwell (Mossad). Dorril says virtually nothing of substance about the role of journalists as disseminators of disinformation for the purposes of influencing domestic politics. Pity. It may well be, however, that this chapter was savagely cut by libel lawyers: it certainly reads unevenly. Another possibility is that he is closely reliant on assets: in his list of acknowledgements I counted nine who I regard in this light (p.x/xi). The idea of journalists acting as 'outriders' for the secret state (including Special Branch) isn't one that Lustgarten and Ian Leigh entertain at all, seriously believing of stories in the so-called 'quality press' that they are "neither more nor less reliable than other reportage of current political developments" (p.xi). That said, Chapter 10 of their book makes many useful points about the media/state relationship nonetheless. My own experience of journalists is that the vast majority are shallow, politically illiterate, cowardly,

lazy and venal. There are honourable exceptions, but they stand out like diamonds among a dung-heap. Supposedly 'liberal' papers like the *Guardian* and *Independent* are no better than the rest, in some respects worse.

33 According to Adams, this story worried her so much that she moved the same day it appeared: nonetheless having had advance notice, unlike most fingered in the media (*op. cit.* p.103). In one recent trial of English IRA members (on which more below), Rimington's address was (allegedly) found (*Today* 15/4/94). The MI5-SB conflict is examined in Stephen Dorril *op. cit.* p.235-53, and see also (for example) *Daily Telegraph* 19/4/92 and the *Guardian* 11/3/93. Dorril takes a position far more supportive of Special Branch/the police generally than MI5: I'd rather not adjudicate between them thank you very much.

34 *Belfast Telegraph* 3/11/93.

35 22/12/93 p.18-20.

Welsh nationalism — repeating the Irish scenario?

THE FIRST AREA of MI5 activity in recent times to be looked at is their operation against *Meibion Glyndwr*, the Welsh holiday home arsonists.[1] Throughout the course of their campaign, there has been persistent speculation that *Meibion Glyndwr* has been linked to all sorts of people with whom they would have no truck — MI5 themselves and the now-defunct Official National Front. While it is not a subject I will dwell on here, I have little time for that fantasy, which says far more about those propagating it than *MG* themselves.[2] The whole course of *MG*'s post-1988 campaign deserves analysis at some point, for there does seem to have been a qualitative shift, not least to targets outside Wales, but this is not the time or the place for that. Suffice to say that as far back as 1982 MI5 showed a keen interest in Welsh Nationalists presumed to be associated with *MG*.[3]

In a trial of alleged MG activists, that lasted from January to March 1993 one of the defendants, twenty year old Sion Roberts was found guilty of sending four incendiary devices to prominent Tories and police officers. It was revealed, thanks to the refusal of the trial judge to be intimidated into suppressing it, that starting in September 1991 as many as *38 MI5 operatives* had placed him and two others under surveillance. The defence argument was that he and the others had been framed by MI5; planting bomb-making equipment in his flat, and themselves sending the devices through the post that Roberts was blamed for[4]

During the trial (rumoured to have cost £7 million although the official figure given was £1 million)[5] the jury was vetted, the first time this has been acknowledged as occurring since 1978.[6] There was no evidence put forward by the prosecution to indicate any of the three were members of *Meibion Glyndwr*, an organisation that has thus successfully eluded state attention since 1979. Not only was Roberts not initially charged with posting the explosives, he was only found guilty after a police witness had stated on oath in court that he had allegedly seen Roberts delivering the devices to the home of another defendant. The political implications of the case for Wales have been adequately dwelt on elsewhere.[7] Roberts' appeal against his conviction, heard in late July 1994 at the Old Bailey, failed, as one might have expected given the extraordinary lengths gone to in order to secure a conviction in the first place.

The case was important for a number of reasons. For a start, the fact that even a jury picked to be unsympathetic should acquit all three defendants of the charge of 'conspiracy', with its political overtones, shows how much work MI5 still have to do to convince a broader public of the sinister nature of militant Welsh nationalism. Also, as Lustgarten & Leigh point out, without the burglary by MI5 to ostensibly plant bugs, which led to the finding (or in my view planting) of material evidence, the police wouldn't have been able to bring charges. Had the police broken in, any evidence obtained would have been ruled inadmissible in court. A strange state of affairs then, when the prime contribution of MI5, taking things at face-value, was to use methods to obtain evidence that only an unaccountable supralegal body like MI5 can hope to get away with.[8] A more general point is that from an MI5 point of view, framing an innocent young man (Roberts) was highly effective. By 'criminalising' a strand of militant Welsh nationalism this rank injustice will have heightened opposition, amongst those already politicised, to English rule, thus leading to increased 'subversion' to monitor. According to an acute observer from the Celtic League, the "parallel with the North of Ireland is an almost perfect match. In the early 1970's MI5 personnel were seconded into the province to deal with the alleged inadequacies of the 'native' police. Their remit to gather intelligence on paramilitary bodies gained a momentum which was to lead to allegations (many subsequently substantiated) of involvement between recruited criminals and MI5 officers in an orgy of deceit, robbery and murder".[9] Since that trial, Welsh nationalists have been subject to further unwelcome state attention. In the first such prosecution since 1974 (of alleged IRA members for wearing 'political uniforms' at a funeral), seven Welsh militants were arrested in July 1993 under the same section of the 1936 Public Order Act for their part in the annual *Abergele* parade to commemorate the deaths of Alwyn Jones/George Taylor.[10] The seven called themselves the *Meibion Glyndwr* colour party, and the prosecution argued they were thereby associated with the illegal *MG* group. When the case came to trial in April 1994, the court found them guilty, despite a statement by a police Inspector that he had "no idea" who *MG* are.[11] Despite being found guilty, the seven were given conditional discharges — a 'leniency' which cleverly denied them further publicity *and* kept the threat of further state action hanging over them, in order to hinder any protests they might (hypothetically) have been planning to celebrate in appropriate style the 25th anniversary of Charles' Investiture. The guilty verdict will also serve to legitimise further interference by the state in the personal lives of the defendants and their associates — thus widening the 'shooting gallery' of MI5 targets and clearing the way for further framings.[12] The use of legislation last applied against Irish Republicans is a chilling pointer to the future tactics and strategy MI5 are considering in Wales — we shall see.[13]

For the moment, there seems to have been a marked downturn in *MG* activity, notwithstanding the call in December 1993 by *Cayo Evans* (formerly of the 1960's outfit the Free Welsh Army) for more actions including violence.[14] The downturn is quite likely to have been due to the marked decline in holiday homes in Wales, itself partly due to the success of *MG's* earlier campaign as well as the recession.[15] It is reasonable to anticipate that if and when there is an upturn in *MG* activity, MI5 operatives will be to the fore, whether entrapping, fitting people up again or maybe even carrying out actions is something that time will reveal.

Notes:

1 The words mean 'Sons of Glyndwr', *Owain Glyndwr* being a fifteenth century prince who rebelled against English rule. The name is particularly apt because although *Glyndwr's* revolt was ultimately unsuccessful, he was never captured.

2 See for example John Merritt/Tony Heath 'NF linked to Welsh arson campaign' the *Observer* 9/10/88. A conventional summary of the campaign to date (which in my view correctly rejects the idea of NF-*MG* links) is that by Paul Mercer in the *British Directory of Political Organisations* Longman 1994.

3 See *City Limits* (London) 12/2/82.

4 See for example reports of the trial in the *Independent* (15/1/93), *Western Mail* (20/1/93), (Liverpool) *Daily Post* (21/1/93, 26/1/93, 28/1/93), *Caernarfon Herald* (29/1/93). The verdict was covered in the *Daily Post, Daily Telegraph, Guardian, Independent* and *Western Mail* for 10/3/93. Specific mention must be made of the article by Richard Norton-Taylor in the *Guardian* after the trial had ended, which for me crossed the boundary between reportage and disinformation. I object to his retailing the MI5 (for-public-consumption) version of events as though it was *fact*, ending up by saying "the question remains whether MI5's undercover activities helped to quash a potentially more serious and violent threat, or whether the disclosure of its presence will prove counterproductive in an area of nationalist support" (p.4). 'Counterproductive' for who we might ask — the legitimacy of the English state? Or maybe the public image of MI5? This trial and the MI5 operation that engendered it raises, for those genuinely concerned about the malevolent activities of the secret state, far different and more urgent questions than the ones Norton-Taylor asked. Norton-Taylor himself, as the only full-time 'security service' correspondent on any newspaper, is someone worth talking about. Undoubtedly, his newspaper articles contain a wealth of useful information, of great use to anyone studying the secret state, and he (legitimately) derives a lot of it from close contact with their operatives/spin-doctors. However, this has a price — he works for a paper which rigidly respects the 'D' notice system, accepts the rights of the secret state to continue to exist, and always ducks (at best) the key political questions raised by the antics of the secret state. Indicative of both his good and bad points is the (useful) book he wrote for the NCCL (Liberty), *In Defence of The Realm? The case for Accountable Secret Services* (1990). While it includes a page on journalists subject to hostile MI5 attention, (just like Dorril) there is nothing on them as willing carriers of MI5 disinformation — when even Adams has that. Norton-Taylor's association with/uncritical utilisation of the nefarious *Searchlight* magazine also brings his judgement into question: he was to my knowledge the only journalist to preview the joint *World In Action/Searchlight* production on Combat 18 of 19/4/93 (see the *Guardian* 19/4/93).

5 *Wales on Sunday* 5/6/94.

6   Philip Thomas, 'Secret Police on Trial' *Planet* 98 April/May 1993 p.7.

7   See *Y Faner Goch* (Wrecsam) 48 p.1/4 1993, *CARN* (the splendid and always highly informative journal of the Celtic League) issue 81 (p.23), 82 (p.11) and 83 (p.11) — all 1993.

8   *Op. cit.* p.384.

9   *CARN* 84 Winter 1993-4 p.23.

10   These men were killed in 1969 when a bomb they were transporting exploded prematurely, this one the same day as Charles was invested as 'Prince of Wales'.

11   *Guardian* 8/4/94. In which case, perhaps the Inspector could communicate this to to those responsible for keeping *Sion Roberts* in prison? And as a matter of interest, two of the defendants are brothers of Roberts.

12   One of the defendants in the earlier trial, David Davies, had been 'fitted up' using as pretext his membership of the 1991 *MG* colour party.

13   The article by Owen Bowcott in the *Guardian* 7/4/94 (Section 2 p.10-11) is, despite cynical traces, a good and interesting piece.

14   *Wales on Sunday* 12/12/93.

15   See *Wales on Sunday* 24/4/94 p.1-3 and *CARN* 86 Summer 1994 p.12.

Scottish nationalism — the ghost at the banquet?

IF THE ACTIVITIES of *Meibion Glyndwr* have received extensive MI5 but little *public* attention in England, the actions of militant Scottish Nationalists such as the 'Scottish National Liberation Army' appear at first sight to have received even less of either.[1] At the previous peak of SNLA activity, in 1983, Adam Busby (Operations Officer) escaped to Dublin, where he has remained ever since. His one-time colleague, David Dinsmore, also escaped (jumping bail) in 1983, and finally returned to Scotland to 'face the music' on letter-bombing charges in October 1993.[2] Reports of his return in the Scottish press gave a hint as to how MI5 would like us to believe they view Scottish nationalism of the incendiary kind: it was said that in 1983 (and we can speculate subsequently) "MI5's involvement . . . stopped short of 'hands-on' activity, however. Scottish nationalist terrorism was low on MI5's list of priorities with the IRA and foreign terror groups active".[3]

The allegedly low importance attached to militant Scottish nationalism by the secret state and Special Branch sits ill, however, with the still unexplained murder of veteran Scottish Nationalist Willie McRae in April 1985, and the 1984 allegations that there were links between the SNLA and the Irish National Liberation Army (INLA).[4] This murder has been persuasively linked to the secret state.[5] The SNLA, with which McRae was (among other things) associated[6] had, until recently, a very elusive profile. All this was to dramatically change in March 1993, for starting on 7/3, for a period of three months, one Andrew McIntosh (along with unknown others), carried out a campaign of bombings, involving mortars and the traditional letter variety, both hoax and otherwise. He was eventually caught because he loaned his car to two activists from the anti-English group 'Settler Watch', and they were espied sticking up posters by an 11 year old boy, who informed the police, resulting in the car being traced. McIntosh was then put under surveillance, and although this revealed little, he was arrested on 28/8/93, and at his home a (functional) ARM 30 Kalashnikov rifle (reputedly of Iraqi or Egyptian origin) and an arsenal of other weapons and ammunition was found. When the case came to trial, he was found guilty and sentenced to 12 years imprisonment.[7]

Although there was no public hint MI5 had ever been involved in the investigation, and the media presented him as an 'isolated crank', the incongruities in the case may be highly significant. The first thing that seems strange is when the actions began Adam Busby is reported to have said "it is not the SNLA. We have no connection with this but we thoroughly approve of it".[8] This might cast doubt on *later* claims by Busby that the whole thing was pre-planned.[9] Sources close to the SNLA have speculated that Busby may have initially denied knowledge of McIntosh's activities as part of a 'intelligence blank', to safeguard organisational integrity. The second thing of note concerns the media allegation that as well as being a member of various Scottish Nationalist groups, according to a fellow-member of the Aberdeen shooting club said of him, he is alleged to have "boasted of having connections with the UDA in Belfast and inevitably wore a blue denim jacket with a Red Hand of Ulster on the front".[10] Other sources have strongly denied McIntosh had any Ulster Loyalist connections, instead describing him as as a long-time supporter of Irish Republicanism, so we have two diametrically opposed contentions there. The Parachute Regiment (reservist) background of McIntosh is rather more easily explained: he is likely to have joined to get 'technical' knowledge. McIntosh's reticence when interrogated is likely to have been due to a strong commitment, likewise his refusal to offer a defence at the trial, which ended in him getting a 12 year sentence.

Thus far, I have been working on the assumption he may well have been guilty (technically) of the charges laid against him. An article in *CARN* questions this, pointing out the bulk of the evidence against McIntosh was 'confessional', not forensic (which leaves aside the question of weaponry/ammunition found at his home . . .). Further, the crucial 'confession' was not obtained in the police station, on tape, as is standard practice, but written down in a notebook by only one police officer. Even more strangely, if the Inspector's notes of the 'interview' are correct, he didn't even ask McIntosh who else might have been involved in the alleged SNLA activities. The only two witnesses against McIntosh were the police officers he allegedly confessed to, and the judge had to go to great lengths to convince the jury police evidence was to be taken at face value.[11] Curiouser and curiouser! Given it is not known who else McIntosh was involved with operationally, the book will have to remain open on the extent (if any) of MI5 involvement in his arrest. At present, the publicly available evidence points to the local police (CID, not even Special Branch). He was charged with the grosser crime of 'conspiracy' rather than just with firearms offences, which is what Special Branch would most likely have charged him with on their own, leading to a lesser sentence. This may just indicate some higher level involvement by the British state in the prosecution of this case. But such a charge may also indicate uniformed-Special Branch rivalry too. There have been reports (not in the press) that while in custody McIntosh was questioned by a London-based officer 'attached to Special Branch' (a euphemism for MI5)[12] about a number of matters, including Willie McRae. This would indicate the McRae case is still a 'live' issue for the secret state, as well it might be. MI5 may, therefore, have been involved in targeting McIntosh, and this might explain the ambitious charges brought against him, just as in the Roberts case. A scant regard for the law as it relates to their own activities seems to go hand in hand with MI5 adopting a 'hard line' towards those opponents they decide to deal with in the courts rather than by other means.

Notes:

1   Perhaps this is due to a general news black out of SNLA activities, which has however, never been total even up to the present eg see *Sunday Mail* 15/12/91 and 9/2/92 for examples unrelated to matters discussed here. On the other hand (for example), devices planted by the SNLA outside Stonehaven courthouse 27/8/94 and Aberdeen Sherriff's Court 8/9/94 received sparse media coverage. As well as the summary in Mercer *op. cit.* the standard work is Andrew Murray Scott and Iain Macleay *Britain's Secret War: Tartan Terrorism and the Anglo-American State* (Mainstream Press 1990). This last book is very controversial — a review in *CARN* (issue 74 Summer 1991 p.22) described the book (with examples) as "disinformation", stating it is "completely unsafe even for the most simple reference". Also see the critical letter by Malcolm Slesser in *Scotland on Sunday* 21/10/90].

2   For which he was eventually sentenced to 240 hours community service.

3   *The Scotsman* 9/2/94 p.11. Dinsmore's public renunciation of direct action and the light sentence passed led his former comrade in arms Adam Busby to denounce the "shabby deal" whereby he had faced lesser charges (one of conspiracy being dropped). The inference was that Dinsmore might have informed on former SNLA comrades in return (*Glasgow Herald* 9/2/94).

4   See Dorril *op. cit.* p.256-7 who says that it was highly likely MI5 were targetting McRae and Dinsmore as well as the SNLA as a whole.

5   On McRae see *CARN* 61, and also issue 77 Spring 1992 which updates matters. *CARN* 78 covers the bizarre death of Kevin Collison on 9/4/92, as did the Scottish edition of the *Observer* 19/4/92.

6   See *Glasgow Herald* 1/2/92.

7   See *Glasgow Herald* 1/2/92.

8   Cited *Glasgow Herald* 23/12/93 p.9.

9   The line taken by the *Scotsman* 23/12/93.

10 Ibid. p.4 The trial was also covered in editions of the *Scotsman* for 14/12, 18/12, 21/12, 22/12 and 24/12/93. Also see the *Glasgow Herald* for 15/12, 17/12, 18/12 and 22/12/93, as well as the *Daily Record* for 18/12 and 23/12/93.

11 *CARN* 85 Spring 1994 p.4. A less sympathetic view of McIntosh' actions was taken by a contributor to the next issue of *CARN* who took the traditional SNP line that the case "is one of a long line of half-baked 'tartan terrorism' trials which the establishment delights in and has usually fomented when the SNP is on the rise" (issue 86 Summer 1994 p.3).

12 For if they were part of SB then why not admit it? 'Attached to' means not part of, and given there was no reason for a policeman to travel all the way from London to ask about McRae, it is highly likely to have been MI5.

Red Action — new beer in old bottles

DESPITE THE END of the Cold War, MI5 has shown itself well capable of upgrading 'old targets' to fit in with current needs. Something of this nature seems to have occurred with the small but militant far left 'Red Action', some of whose founders were expelled from the Socialist Worker's Party (SWP), but who went on to develop (along with people who had never been in the SWP) a highly distinctive politics. Below, I shall discuss the circumstances surrounding two recent court cases, involved in each of which (among others) were two *different* members of Red Action. In the second case, evidence of MI5 involvement is very clear-cut, not so with the first, which is nevertheless well worthy of analysis in the current context.

The prelude to the first case is two events early in 1993. On the 28th of January, two bombs went off outside Harrods in Central London, slightly injuring four people. On the 3rd of February, two further bombs went off in London, one at South Kensington tube station the other on a train from Victoria to Ramsgate, all claimed by the IRA.[1] This was followed up by the arrests in early March of two *British* suspects (reportedly following a shoot-out) at a house in Stoke Newington, where significant amounts of Semtex explosive, detonators and arms were found.[2] One of the two arrested, Patrick Hayes, was a long-standing member of Red Action (RA), occupying a very prominent position indeed within (London) Anti-Fascist Action. The other, ex-soldier Jan Taylor, is not believed to have been an RA member.

The case is already out of the ordinary, but becomes even more so when we learn that acccording to the *Guardian* report of the arrest, Scotland Yard had possessed video film-footage of the two alleged suspects since January 28th, only releasing the pictures after "an intensive operation to find the men had failed".[3] Given that Patrick Hayes was unquestionably well known to the police because of his role in (entirely legal) anti-fascist activity, for example liasing with police concerning the AFA march through Bethnal Green (East London) in November 1991, I find it very difficult to believe that, had they seen the photographs, police would not have recognised him immediately.[4] All this seems to point to the photographs *not having been shown* to the police personnel likely to have recognised Hayes (at least), and this exclusion, we can reasonably conjecture, would have applied to Special Branch too. Ammunition for this argument is provided by an article from the *Mail on Sunday* political editor 2/5/93, who complained that the Harrod's video stills "were suppressed at the request of MI5 for 33 days". He attributed the delay (charitably) to some fanciful notion that 300 MI5 officers plus 150 Special Branch/Anti-Terrorist Squad officers were hanging around London waiting for these characters to plant other devices — an unlikely story, especially given that with the Victoria-Ramsgate bomb, they seem to have done *precisely* that, without hindrance![5] A further incongruity surrounding the video-footage was illustrated by the *Daily Telegraph* report of the trial, which said that "in the month between the seizure of the Harrods video . . . and its release to the public, investigators checked the video images against files in London, Ulster and Ireland. But the file pictures of the pair were old and, according to one source, the video images 'really didn't register'."[6] The *Guardian* reported that in addition to the Harrod's footage, there was also film of the two men in a branch of WH Smith's "at Victoria station prior to the bomb on the 9.05 Victoria-Ramsgate train on February 3rd".[7]

What we have so far then is a *definite* suppression of the photos from the public domain for 28 days: no further proof of that needed. What we *also* have, is the possibility that this footage (from Harrod's and we must presume WH Smith's) was *deliberately kept* from the police by MI5. Again, the evidence is strong: MI5 are now fully in charge of anti-IRA activity on the mainland, and would unquestionably have taken control of the footage. We also can say, with virtually the same degree of probability, that Hayes at least was *well known* to some police officers by sight, and is *bound* to have featured on the footage of AFA demonstrations those nice police persons in helicopters get their kicks out of filming and passing to the cine-enthusiasts of Special Branch (in the first instance). The remaining (almost rhetorical) question is, would MI5 have had access to the Special Branch picture-library, even before the Harrod's bombing? The answer to that most definitely has to be yes. The only real doubt that might hypothetically arise is the one that *if* MI5 hadn't expected British Leftists to engage in 'active service' for the IRA, they mightn't have thought of Hayes as a possible suspect. Not only does this explanation depend on an assumption (lack of MI5 foreknowledge) that I have some difficulty coming to terms with, it *doesn't* explain why the photo wasn't shown to the police who would have recognised Hayes. Furthermore, since at least July 1992 by their own admission (see below) MI5 agent Patrick Daly had been involved in an attempt to make the INLA operational on the mainland, including *another* member of RA. Additionally, RA themselves have stated their belief that since 'Operation Blackshirt' in November 1991, they have been subject to MI5 surveillance/disruption. These two things make it highly likely that MI5 know who all key RA personnel (like Hayes) are, and would not find incomprehensible the idea of RA members becoming militarily 'operational' for the Republican movement. Looked at another way, suppose we assume for the sake of argument police *did* see the photo, and recognise Hayes. Are we being asked to believe that the police, especially the beleaguered (by MI5) Scotland Yard Anti-Terrorist Squad would have passed up a chance to win back some *kudos* by identifying Hayes at least? Even assuming that wasn't a consideration, the police would need some *reason* for keeping quiet until March. And by far the best way to ensure silence would be an MI5 claim this was necessary because of an operation being mounted in relation to Hayes/Taylor. If the police/SB were shown the photos, somebody would have recognised Hayes for sure: in this case the stupidity of PC Plod is not an explanation I take seriously.

Having established a reasonable probability that MI5 had the video-stills suppressed deliberately, because (most likely) they already knew, shortly after the Harrods bomb if not before, about the identities of Hayes and Taylor, there is still the question of motive. There are a variety that can be imputed, for a start, placing images on TV in a spectacular fashion so as to subconsciously influence potential jurors in advance. This might explain the very charade that was eventually gone through of asking for the public to identify people when the state already knew who they were! Little propaganda to be had out of just a short news item announcing their arrest — the 'search' for Hayes/Taylor was an ideal pretext for a media spectacular. This explains the eventual showing of the pictures, but *not* the extent of the delay in showing them. Another motive for suppression, which I tend to favour most, is that MI5 *wanted* Hayes and Taylor to carry out further actions after Harrod's (if not earlier) so *didn't want* them to be caught straight away. In this scenario, the more bombs Hayes/Taylor planted, and logically the more casualties, the *better* it would be. That license was (hypothetically) given to the two to plant such bombs goes to the heart of just what MI5's current strategy may be, and the rationale behind it, as well as difficult questions about the extent of MI5 penetration of the IRA itself, and the purposes of such.

Those questions I will return to, but alternative possibilities more in keeping with MI5's declared role of 'fighting Irish terrorism' need to be evaluated first. One defence of MI5 might be that, having been identified, Hayes/Taylor were placed under surveillance, in order to see if anyone else was involved, this explaining the delay in arresting them. A problem with this explanation is that it doesn't account for why they were apparently allowed to place the bombs on the Victoria to Ramsgate train/at South Kensington tube station. Contemporary press reports do not indicate a closely-watching MI5 team concerned above all to prevent loss of civilian life — speaking of the Victoria bomb the *Times* said that after the phoned warning "police had no time to stop it [the train] before it left the station. It was nearly a quarter of an hour before the warning was passed to Network SouthEast, who managed to stop the train at . . . Beckenham" (4/2/93). This lack of concern for casualties, and disinterest in prevention, might be seen as consistent with the pro-active *encouraging* role I see MI5 as taking in regard to political violence. A fall-back defence for them here might be that it took more than a few days to scan through data bases to find out who Hayes/Taylor were. Even assuming this to be possible (as it is) then why didn't the state wait even longer? Thirty-three days isn't a long time to place people under surveillance: six months is more likely a standard period. Time and again though, we come back to the recurring problem: even assuming MI5 wouldn't have recognised Hayes immediately, the police *would have*, just as they (or members of the public) did within minutes of the publicity in early March. An indicator that something was being covered up was the comment in the *Daily Telegraph* that both of them — ie Taylor *and* Hayes, "faded from police interest in the mid-1980's" (14/5/94). This is patently untrue in Hayes' case, as we have seen, therefore somebody wanted to cover something up by circulating this tale in the public domain.

So, I'm saying here that I think MI5 already knew the identities of Hayes and Taylor at least as far back as the Harrod's bomb in January 1993. Conjecture on whether MI5 is likely to have known about them beforehand is necessarily highly speculative, but worthwhile. Red Action themselves are well aware of questions raised by the actions of Hayes and Taylor, including those along the lines of "Were they recruited by the IRA, or did they make the initial approach? If in fact they volunteered their services, how, the media wondered, did they earn the IRA's trust?"[8] While understanding perfectly well Red Action's unwillingness to be drawn into discussing such matters, about which there is no reason to suppose they know anything anyway, there are broader issues of interest here concerning the rest of us on the Left/Green axis. I think it is too restrictive of RA to imply these are just questions of interest to the media: if the overall analysis of MI5 strategy in this book is right, the above are questions of great relevance to all radical political activists, not least to prevent repetition.

The motivations of Hayes and Taylor for their involvement in IRA activity are straightforward, political commitment, and Hayes' speech from the dock is a traditional hardline Republican one, in which the root cause of their campaign was seen as stemming from the British state's 1969 "armed response to the political process in the North". He dismissed the criminal charges laid against him as invalid, seeing the issues at stake in the trial as *political* in nature, and himself an IRA volunteer — ie a soldier engaged in a war. Far from seeking to minimise his involvement, Hayes admitted to planting bombs at Canary Wharf, Tottenham Court Road and Woodside Park, as well as driving a Volvo lorry bomb in Stoke Newington 14/11/92 with which he had not been charged, and for which another man Patrick Kelly, is at present languishing in jail.[9] According to Hayes, and he would know, Kelly has no connection with the IRA, and I am well inclined to believe Kelly's present incarceration is yet another fit-up of an innocent man by the British legal system. Back to the point, the commitment/beliefs of Hayes/Taylor are not in doubt (while of course retaining my own opinions on the advisability of their course of action) — what interests me is their *timing*. Put simply, given that RA have always had a line of militant verbal support for the armed Republican cause, two things need to be explained: why Hayes (and indeed Liam Heffernan mentioned below) should have decided to become operational when they did, and why it had not happened to them (or any other RA members) earlier. Simply seeing IRA activity as a consequence of their overall political ideology, as though timing wasn't an important consideration, as did both *Red Action* and the *Guardian* report (14/5/94), doesn't address the pertinent question, in my view. This question *was* addressed in that favourite 'spook' paper the *Daily Telegraph* (14/5/94), and I will return to that in a moment.

The mode of operation of Hayes/Taylor yields few firm clues as to their exact relationship with the IRA higher ecehelons, but it is worth examining, not from a 'police' point of view, but in terms of analysing MI5 strategy. That not just Semtex but also two AK47s and two hand-guns were found in Hayes' flat, and in total Hayes admitted to having disposed of a full seven tons of home-made explosive, indicates their involvement was no casual affair.[10] I find it unusual that any experienced IRA unit would keep weapons/explosives in their place of residence, though such has happened before for short periods. The explosive (fertilizer mix) was of the same sort that devastated the City of London early in 1993, and the failure of any of the three fertiliser bombs planted by Hayes to fully ignite shouldn't detract from the potency of the mixture — it is a very hit and miss affair with such material, apparently. The *Guardian* did find it "strange that a unit producing sophisticated bombs capable of massive damage were unaware of the possibility of security cameras in stations and outside potential targets" (14/5/94). I do too, slightly, and it must be remembered that their activities were highly novel — the first English-born 'Active Service Unit' (ASU), and the first IRA operatives to place bombs on a train outside Ireland.[11] It is far easier to recount reasons as to why Hayes and Taylor were *unlikely* to be used by the IRA than as to why they might be. Not just their country of birth, but also Taylor's British army past, Hayes' membership of a far left group, particularly one that in the past had a close relationship with the Irish Republican Socialist Party, closely aligned to the INLA.[12] The idea of the IRA using people in their ASUs who are already well known to the British police for anti-fascist activity/Republican sympathies is also highly unusual, although not unique — for instance the case of Nick Mullen.[13] The reasons for past reticence on the IRA's part have been virtually a mirror-image of why Loyalists have previously been similarly reticent in dealings with British fascists — a fear members of such groups are 'play-acting' and in any case riddled with police agents. This latter allegation is precisely one that has been hurled against RA itself, and will be returned to below.

What I'm saying about the activities of Hayes and Taylor is this: the *timing* is crucial, why then and not earlier. Suspicion that their activities may have (despite them not knowing it) fitted into a state agenda (as well as an IRA one) is fuelled by the 33 day suppression of the photographs. Returning to motive, and mechanism, it seems likely that the answer might lie somewhere inside the IRA. There are two possible reasons why the IRA might have decided it could use Hayes and Taylor. The first is that given the ASU's active in England adhere to a cell structure, any possible risk occasioned by liasing with British Leftists would have been minimised — maybe only *one* person needs to have had contact with them. If the ASU was not in contact with any other ASUs, the worse that could have happened the loss of a quantity of weaponry/explosives (the latter of which may have been obtained by Hayes/Taylor in

England anyway). That no members of the 'Brit Left' had been operational before might have led IRA strategists to think this was yet another way to remain one step ahead of the British state, as a feature of the IRA's campaign has been their ability to change tactics unexpectedly time and again. In this scenario, the possible political effects in England of using British Leftists in military actions would not have been a significant factor in IRA thinking. All of the above I concede, but there is a second reason, which in practice might well have co-existed along with the first. This is that, in line with MI5 strategy, they got one or more of their agents within the IRA to suggest abandoning, or support the removal of, the previous taboo concerning the British far left. There would have been no particular need for MI5 assets to have monitored in detail the actual recruitment of Hayes/Taylor, indeed far better for them not to have done. Given there are very few on the British Left who *would* contemplate becoming active on behalf of the IRA/INLA, then picking such people up back in England would be a relatively easy task. In this situation, the 'danger' of English Leftists becoming labelled as terrorists would be far easier to convince say the government of, if they were allowed license (even if under constant surveillance) to carry out actions: for instance the Victoria-Ramsgate bomb at least.

The advantages for MI5 of expanding the range of those who could thereby be legitimately regarded as 'terrorist' targets, is obvious and a point I will return to constantly. The chief battle-ground for this is not the media, but nevertheless one might have expected to see it surface there somewhere. So it turned out: as sure as night follows day, as if in accordance with a pre-ordained script, at the end of March 1993 the press carried three articles describing the belief of 'Security Chiefs' that the "IRA has recruited bombers for its terrorist campaigns in mainland Britain from supporters of extreme Left-wing organisations".[14] The other side of this coin is, as we shall see, Loyalist-Fascist links. It wasn't just Red Action that was targetted, two articles mentioned unspecified 'anarchist' groups, but Red Action was most prominently featured.[15] The inclusion of anarchist groups alongside Red Action was no accident: as we shall see below, the anarchist milieu has too been subject to extensive state/*agent provocateur* attention in recent times also. Perhaps the next gambit is an anarchist-ALF-IRA triangle, to complete the set of criss-crossing 'connections'.

Notes:

1 See *The Times* 4/2/93.
2 I have heard from one source a bizarre tale that along with the two named below, there was a *third* person at the house when the police arrived, allegedly an Irish *Sinn Fein* member, who is supposed to have been the person who fired the shots at police. If such a person does exist, and was there doing such things, it beggars belief that they weren't arrested and charged, raising all sorts of troubling questions. I do not *know* that such a person exists, and there is no hard evidence for it, the only possible corroboration being

(indirectly) provided by the *Guardian* report of the arrest speaking of *three* persons captured. But then, given journalists inability to add up is as legendary as their general lack of interest in truth, this hardly counts as 'proof'.

3   3/3/93, written by Lawrence Donegan and John Mullin.

4   Two people of my acquaintance, who unlike me *have* met Hayes, say the minute they saw his photo on the front covers of the *Standard/Daily Mirror* (1/3/93), it was clear just who it *might* be.

5   Other reports, perhaps significantly, make no comment as to *who* ordered the suppression of the photos for such a length of time, yet surely this would be a pertinent question to raise, given the time-lapse between the Harrods/train bombs and the arrests (see *Evening Standard* 13/5/94, *Daily Telegraph* 14/5/94, *Guardian* 14/5/94). There is also the question of the other activities admitted to by Hayes from at least November 15th 1992: starting with the Canary Wharf bomb (see his court-room speech, reproduced in *Red Action* 68 Summer 1994 p.1). An extremely interesting episode of the fictional drama series 'The Chief' (about a radical Chief Constable), *did* ask the hard questions in a programme screened mid-1993. In the story, video footage of an IRA Active Service Unit planting a bomb in a shopping centre is stolen by MI5 from the local force, much to the annoyance of the Chief, and suppressed. Subsequently, a bomb goes off on a train, in which thankfully few are hurt, but he is most displeased at having to take the rap for MI5, given the second bomb is blamed on him for not having caught the suspects: suspects who were allowed to continue in their activity because the cell had been thoroughly penetrated by MI5. An intriguing storyline — perhaps somebody was trying to say something here??.

6   'Long Held assumptions shattered by arrests' (John Steele 'Courts Correspondent' 14/5/94).

7   14/5/94.

8   *Red Action* issue 68 Summer 1994 p.1.

9   All this from Red Action 68 Summer 1994 p.1.

10   See *Guardian* 14/5/94 and *Red Action* 68 p.1 on this.

11   According to the *Times* 4/2/93.

12   All points made in the *Daily Telegraph* 14/5/94.

13   A Leftist who was jailed at the Old Bailey in 1990 for 30 years on charges of assisting a mainland IRA ASU. In his case too, explosives and arms were found, but the address used was not his, and the owners were unaware of the use to which the property was being put. Another point to note is that he was (allegedly) acting in a support role only, and involved no other British Leftists (see *Daily Telegraph* 9/6/90 and the earlier report on press activity prior to his trial in *Workers Press* 29/2/90). The case was also subject to a bizarre attempt to concoct an ANC:IRA link out of his presence in Zimbabwesee 'The IRA's Mr Fixit pays a visit', *Daily Telegraph* 1/7/90, by Valerie Elliot, (the late) Simon O'Dwyer and Fred Bridgland (two of them names to watch out for on Jackanory). Mullen's comment on their endeavours was printed in the *Daily Telegraph* 15/7/90.

14   *Sunday Telegraph* 28/3/93, also *Sunday Times* 28/3/93, this last written by Ian Birrell and John Davison, these same two journalists having been involved in the bogus 'Insight' investigation that speciously targetted Liverpool Militant leader Derek Hatton (see *Sunday Times* 24/1/93 for example), *Daily Express* 2/4/93 entitled 'IRA's Red Brigade' (written

by John Burns and Norman Luck). See also the item 'MI5 banks on Cold War Skills' in the *Times* 27/4/93 written by Defence Correspondent Michael Evans.

15   Also receiving a guest-mention in a nasty piece written by Anthony Walton for the *Daily Star* 10/5/93 which as well as helpfully listing outlets for *Republican News*, complete with photographs, stressed that it was on sale "alongside left-wing papers like Red Action". Red Action's own view that they are being persecuted is partly outlined in issue 64 of *Red Action* December 1992 p.3-4. Information received by me suggests that 'Operation Blackshirt' is not an overall code name for an ongoing campaign against RA, rather it was the name given by the local police hierarchy to the attempts to prosecute RA and (ostensibly) *Searchlight* editor Gerry Gable for affray in 1991. The person who chose the name was a police officer rather more to the right than Left of centre. In any event, his opinions, and determination to prosecute, counted for nothing when it came to it: it is my belief *Searchlight* used their MI5 connections to get the case dropped even before witnesses for the prosecution had finished presenting their case. I further believe the case was only allowed to get to trial in order to facilitate the gathering of further and current information on RA by Gable and his *Searchlight* team (see *At War With The Truth* Mina 1993 footnote 6 pages 26-7).

Why Red Action, & what next?

MY BASIC THESIS is that, to job-create at least, MI5 have been intent on pushing all kinds of groups in a 'terrorist' direction, on all sides of the spectrum, and if the groups/individuals targetted don't 'play ball', setting them up anyway. That said, it needs to be explained why Red Action *specifically* were chosen, after all groups like the 'Revolutionary Communist Party' (RCP) are, at least rhetorically, just as committed to supporting Republicans in what they too see as the 'Irish War'. In practice however, groups like the RCP are harmless, much of their political activity consisting of invading TV studio debates/the meetings of other Left groups and parrotting prepared irrelevant speeches.[1] Red Action provide a great contrast, for not only have they uncompromisingly supported the IRA/INLA in general terms,[2] they have also played a key role in anti-fascist street politics for over a decade, indeed some founder-members were expelled from the Socialist Workers Party (SWP) over this issue in 1982, and are the mainstay of the group most committed to 'physical force' in the anti-racist arena, Anti-Fascist Action.[3] That RA are, therefore, a group committed, in their terms, to 'doing the business' at 'the rougher end of the political market', encompassing two areas of MI5 concern, Ireland and anti-fascism, makes them an obvious target.[4] By going for RA, MI5 can thereby seek to criminalise militant anti-fascism, and maybe AFA itself, by stressing (non-existent) 'operational links' between AFA and Irish Republicans.

So, it is easy to see why Red Action were subject to close state attention of an active sort, the precise *timing* of which is related to MI5's overall strategy. For some in Scotland Yard's 'Anti-Terrorist Squad', annoyed at MI5's nudging them into oblivion, Red Action being 'of interest' might well have provided a pretext for an intra-state 'settling of scores'. Thus, in early March 1993, just after the arrests of the Harrods bomb suspects, a North London flat was stormed by the Squad, and five people arrested under the Prevention of Terrorism Act. One of them was a friend of Stella Rimington's daughter, Sophie Rimington, who it has been suggested (although opinions differ here) knew people on the fringes of Red Action . . . Subsequently, the Metropolitan Police paid £6,000 compensation to each of the three arrested.[5] Three Red Action members, living near to the house raided with such publicity, were (one source has suggested) arrested detained and questioned under the PTA for a number of days, then released. Thus, the raid on Rimington's friend may have been a mistake: or something deliberate that could be *presented* as a mistake by police after the event.

Taken together all these things (along with the Criminal Justice Bill) point to an attempted 'criminalisation' of a section of the British Left, made all the more easy because few, even on the Left itself, have dared comment on it.[6]

In November 1993, *World In Action* did yet another documentary, this time on 'Anti-Fascist Action' (AFA). It is my understanding that, although an arms-length job, much the same people were involved as had produced the April show on Combat 18.[7] In the documentary, AFA was described (in the words of London AFA) as a "full-blown paramilitary conspiracy with a 'cell structure' . . . a 'terrorist' organisation".[8] Red Action came in for some stick towards the end of the entertainment, but I got the distinct impression this was an *opening* shot in the televisual propaganda war against RA, to be followed by more later. London AFA ended their critical review of the programme with the rhetorical question to *World In Action*: "Who's pulling your strings eh?". In my view, as regards matters such as this, the answer is clear — MI5, hence the new name that I would like given wider currency, along with a refusal to co-operate in any way with the crew involved — *MI5 In Action*. Some preliminary remarks about *MI5 In Action* are contained in *A Lie Too Far* and *At War With The Truth*, but I fully intend to examine *MI5IA* in detail at a later date. Hard evidence and leads to follow up on *MI5IA* I'd be grateful to readers for.

The pot has been kept bubbling in media terms with small items like that in the *News of The World* (30/1/94), referring to Red Action as a "London-based paramilitary group . . . blamed for two bombings on London Underground".[9] The far-right 'Pro-Fascist Action' (now the 'Searchlight Victims' Support Group') also got in on the act, producing a sticker stating "Anti-Fascist Action are a front for the IRA. Already three AFA members are under arrest for bombing offences. AFA is a terrorist group . . . BAN IT!"

Whether the true role of MI5 in the above matters will ever fully reach the light of day — that's a difficult question. There is the possibility that MI5 might have agent(s) inside the IRA, pushing them to involve British Leftists to coincide with a state-sponsored Brit agenda. The reaction by Red Action in their paper to the jailing of Hayes and Taylor, while understandable, is one that is going to secure them continuing, and even escalated, MI5 attention. They speak of 'two traditions' on the Left. Revolutionary politics in Britain they write off as being, "and seen to be, counterfeit . . . reformist in ambition and opportunist in approach". Red Action describe themselves as being fully in line with the revolutionary (ie Irish insurrectionary) approach instead. There are two things to say about this position. The first is that MI5 will use it to justify targetting anyone in the periphery of Red Action/Anti-Fascist Action as thereby linked to an 'insurrectionary' (ie 'terrorist') organisation. The second observation is that not only is this dismissal of the struggles of the rest of the far left absurdly sectarian, it doesn't really accord with RA's own practice. The same issue of the paper (68) carries accounts of anti-fascist work such as leafletting in the Isle of Dogs, and an imaginative disruption by RA of seminars aimed at helping employers sack people more easily.

Neither of these issues (for example) are *reducible* to an Irish dimension, therefore RA's own practice is wider than that suggested on page 1. As for Ireland itself, to disagree with the current status quo doesn't necessarily imply support for the IRA/INLA.

Whatever the specifics of RA's position on Ireland, the persecution of RA is not just a matter for their own members, it has knock-on effects across the whole extra-parliamentary Left, which is exactly why, whatever criticisms may be levelled at this or that aspect of their politics, they deserve support for being under attack by the state and their media lackeys. At time of writing, information received suggests the BBC documentary series *Panorama* are planning to 'do a number' on Red Action — if so, I hardly think the full truth will be forthcoming from that quarter, more likely the second instalment of the '*MI5 In Action* job on AFA.[10] A recent book on the INLA, *Deadly Divisions* (by Jack Holland & Henry McDonald) contains a disturbing allegation about RA, that "several former INLA activists claimed that Red Action had been penetrated by the British secret services and used to spy on Republican groups in the North and the Republic"[11] Henry McDonald later stated that "former leader Jimmy Brown told me shortly before he was killed that he distrusted Red Action. He said he believed they were run by British Intelligence".[12] These are very disturbing allegations, and a number of points can be made in response. Firstly, one of the authors (McDonald) is described as a 'security correspondent for the BBC in Northern Ireland', and as such couldn't continue in his job there without close alignment with one branch or other of the state, therefore he is hardly an impartial witness. To quote as your only named source someone who is now (conveniently) dead doesn't help matters: is there any proof Brown, in any case a leader of the rival IPLO, said this, and if he did, what was *his* proof? The account of Brown given in their own book doesn't show him as a reliable source on anything: he not only encouraged one IPLO member to become an informant for RUC Special Branch, and then had him executed for such, he was also the guiding light behind IPLO drug-dealing — an activity strongly condemned by Red Action and others.[13] So, Brown is not a 'credible witness' of anything, not least the alleged state links of others. It is not for me to comment on the book as a whole, but I find it significant that despite having a chronology that goes up to February 1994, and a interview with the INLA March 1994, there is *not a mention* of Daly or the Westbury set-up (never mind the earlier one in 1984). If Holland/McDonald don't mention the activities of a state asset when it had already come out into the public domain by the time of their final manuscript being submitted to the publishers, why should they be taken too seriously on this? All in all there is remarkably little in the book on secret state manipulation of various kinds, for reasons it is easy to guess at. Awaiting further evidence, I regard the throw-away remarks by the authors of this book as yet another instance of the state attack on RA. There is a world of difference between an organisation being *subject to heavy MI5 attention* and one actually *run by them.* Obviously, it is the aspiration of the secret state to be in control of oppositional groups that can then be turned into 'pseudo-gangs' to a greater or lesser degree: below for instance, I will contend that is just what the state is *trying to do* with the spectral neo-nazi 'Combat 18'. The difference between state aspirations and attainment in these matters is measured by the extent of political awareness concerning, and resistance to, such projects. That, I hope to contribute in some small measure to: meanwhile RA deserves support, even if that does not mean endorsing all their politics and behaviour, as well as their unfortunate dismissal of other political tendencies, in particular the things they have said about anarchists at times.

Notes:

1 For example, their disgraceful 'intervention' at the London Statewatch conference April 1993. The rest of their time is spent selling a glossy (and oxymoronic) journal *Living Marxism* to the apparently well-heeled in metropolitan shopping centres, complete with clip-boards and such un-Marxist opening questions as 'Have you got a bank account?'. It is possible though, that elements of the secret state see them as a threat — though I'd have seen them as more of a problem for 'Cultwatch' myself.

2 See for example the *Red Action Irish Newsletter* (Dublin) December 1993 which strongly argued against a Republican cease-fire, and criticised *Sinn Fein's* "lack of political vision".

3 In contrast, the RCP, despite valuable past work (via front organisations such as ELWAR: East London Workers Against Racism), physically defending targets of racist/fascist attack, now adopt a different line. They currently affect to think fascists don't exist, or if they *do* exist, lack any political identity separate from the state/ruling class. This view of fascism, which denies it any independent reality reached a peak of absurdity in the recent statement that the "sole contribution of the BNP to British politics is . . . to serve as a modern reminder of the German Nazis and the Second World War" (*Living Marxism* June 1994 p.5). This downplaying of the possibility of autonomous action on the part of fascists means the RCP are unable to honestly come to terms with fascists when they *do* come across them. Thus it was no surprise to me that upon hearing their 'Irish Freedom March' 7/8/93 may be attacked by fascists, the RCP's 'anti-state' position evaporated. Prior to the event, they welcomed police protection for the march, going so far as to declare (with a touching trust in the 'good faith' of the state) that "police have advised us they'll be stewarding the march very tightly indeed" (*Irish World* 6/8/93). This did not stop the RCP, in a display of breath-taking hypocrisy, complaining about videoing of demonstrators "openly" by police, and promising "now its time to turn the cameras on them . . . we'll be watching you" (*Irish Freedom* Winter 1993 p.21). It is just possible I misinterpreted the RCP here — maybe this was just a passing reference to the fact so many of their members work in the media and they spend so much time time in TV studios debating the non-existence of . . . Speaking still of RCP dishonesty, many who turned up to march did so because they were under the impression it was a (pacifist-inclined) march against 'Militarism' in general, rather than a specifically Irish Republican event. Hardly surprising, given the inaugural meeting of the 'Campaign Against Militarism' (CAM) had been *deliberately* chosen to coincide with that of the already-known CND annual conference, in order to *reduce* the numbers of genuine pacifists who might attend. This

year, presumably to avoid any possible encounters with (non-existent) fascists, the CAM held their August picnic at the proletarian stronghold of Aldermaston instead of central London.

4   RA have also been criticised by others on the Left, see for example the article in *Workers Power* 176 March 1994 p.14 entitled 'Splits Slanders and Sectarianism' which takes a dim view of alleged Red Action manoeuvres within AFA branches, replied to by Red Action in the April issue (p.17). I find the reference in Red Action's reply to "AFA national conference" strange, as to my knowledge there hasn't been one for years: perhaps they meant 'meeting'. Information received from non-partisan sources tends to make me think the greater part of blame in this dispute must be attached to 'Workers Power', for having apparently sought to put out as an AFA leaflet one of their own calling for the liquidation of AFA by alliance with other groups. That Worker's Power have now to all intents and purposes left AFA shows they have little regard for its organisational integrity. Potentially more serious criticism of Red Action tactics, this time in Glasgow AFA, came from the 'Movement for A Scottish Republic' in a circular entitled 'No To The Use Of Violence And Smear Within The Working Class Movement' (n.d. circa November 1993).

5   See the *Guardian* 12/3/93 and 18/8/93, also *Agenda* (NCCL) Summer 1993 p.6-7/9 'When They Come For You In The Morning' covers the experience in one of the victims own words.

6   An honourable exception being the editorial in *Workers Press* (WRP) 3/4/93. This item was surprising (and welcome) because WRP coverage of recent state skull-duggery has been virtually non-existent (as opposed to their excellent 1970's coverage).

7   The lie that Tim "Scargill was responsible for much of the research" for the programme (*Searchlight* February 1994 p.13), which I am in possession of evidence to totally refute, is yet another indication as to who was *really* responsible.

8   *Fighting Talk* 7 Spring 1994 p.7.

9   p.21 Gary Jones was responsible for this piece. Mr Jones featured prominently on a *Panorama* programme (8/8/94) as being allegedly closely involved in Scotland Yard Regional Crime Squad's running of a series of *agents provocateurs*, including (allegedly) playing the part of 'purchaser' of illegal weapons and on another occasion acting as 'paymaster' to an agent, both on behalf of the police. Clearly a public-spirited man who takes his job as 'Crime Correspondent' very seriously, maybe even literally.

10   A telephone call to the Panorama office elicited from them a denial that a programme on Red Action was being planned (5/8/94). By the time you read this, you will probably know the truth of that.

11   p.345, published by *Torc* (Poolbeg Press) Dublin 1994.

12   *Irish World* 3/6/94.

13   *Deadly Divisions* p.311-13.

Welling and after — dog that didn't bark?

ON 16/10/93, the Anti-Nazi League (SWP), in alliance with Youth Against Racism in Europe (Militant), and many others, called a demonstration that was supposed to march on the Welling (Kent) HQ of the BNP, with the intention of getting it shut down. This demonstration, unlike that of the rival Anti-Racist Alliance in Trafalgar Square the same day, was well-attended, the end result being something of a riot, with 19 police officers injured, and an unknown number of demonstrators.[1] After the event, there was the usual hunt for 'extremist infiltrators' who had 'disrupted' the march.[2] The police sought to get even more photographs of the event from various media organisations, obtaining a court order to do so.[3] The judge decided that the 'public interest' far outweighed the potential risk to photographers of them being seen as state agents, effectively.[4] This was to culminate, on 4/2/94, in the release of video film stills showing those demonstrators alleged to have been most responsible.[5] On the face of it, this operation was a straightforward public order matter, but the article in the London *Evening Standard* for 18/10/93, entitled 'Police set to swoop on riot leaders'[6] put it differently. This contained the assertion that Welling had seen "the biggest intelligence operation carried out by police for a demo, with undercover work by Special Branch officers backed by information gathered by MI5 and special police surveillance units". Imminent arrests were promised, to "include a hard core of extremists involved in two militant organisations, Panther UK and Red Action". One key reason this didn't happen is that Red Action were elsewhere, skirmishing with C18 at the Harrow Inn public house in Abbey Wood a few miles away. This would have been well known to the police, who were present there in some numbers,[7] and it is inconceivable that MI5 wouldn't be aware of the encounter. This means that the *Evening Standard* article, containing the only direct reference to MI5, is most likely invention, confusing MI5's *general* interest in Red Action/Panther with a *specific* interest in the events of 16/10.[8] It may also indicate that Panther (who weren't present at Abbey Wood) even more than RA were subject to intense surveillance in a period they were asserting their autonomy from Militant.[9] The logic is: if RA can be labelled 'terrorist' and into anti-fascist violence, then Panther, who also support anti-fascist street tactics can be similarly 'classified'. This recalls the FBI's murderous undercover war on the original US Panthers.[10]

The extensive use of cameras at Welling is no surprise, and it is hard to disagree with Red Action's analysis that the riot was organised by the police, right down to predicting in advance the precise location of the trouble, ensuring it was there that police lines would be weakest.[11] The only other matter worth commenting on is the belief, very widely held in fascist circles, that there is a situation obtaining, as BNP leader John Tyndall put it, whereby, as a cover for their weakness, the government lets "street mobs beat up nationalists and stop their meetings by organised violence while law-enforcement agencies are given the wink to look the other way".[12] The British Movement put the same point more forcefully, arguing that the "red/anarchist freaks actually believe they are fighting the system but really they are controlled by it".[13] Tyndall cites correspondence between (ex-BM leader) Colin Jordan and the Director of Public Prosecutions calling for the prosecution of Anti-Fascist Action for a 1992 TV programme, as well as the precedent of Tyndall's own jailing for breaches of the Public Order Act.[14] A number of points spring to mind here — first, those Leftists who have served/are serving jail sentences for political activity will find this 'alliance' comes as news to them. Secondly, whatever the rhetoric adopted by the ANL, they are hardly up to organising enough force to storm an empty telephone box, therefore to prosecute them for for something they are manifestly incapable of would seem rather unfair.[15] Thirdly, mass demonstrations of the Left (like the Right) can be seen as a useful and largely symbolic political 'safety valve' in most circumstances. Further, the amount of prosecutions against the Far Right for street activity (and even more disseminating racist propaganda) have been very few in number, too, and presumably Tyndall isn't suggesting a conspiracy there? Actions directed against fascists in recent times may well have been aimed at driving them in the direction of illegal activity. But this, I would submit, has not been at the direct behest of the government, but in the interests of fractions of the state apparatus, as outlined above. Recent events in Germany indicate that it is anti-fascists who are being criminalised, for on 5/7/94, 17 activists from *Autonome Anti-Fa*, the most militant anti-fascist group, the equivalent of AFA here, were arrested, and accused of a variety of things, including contact with the virtually non-existent Red Army Fraction. AFA's German counterpart has thus been criminalised: with not a word from 'liberal' commentators here.[16]

Leeds disunited

Outside London, the political atmosphere (violence-wise) is hotting up in a most unpleasant way, nowhere more so than Leeds. There, almost everything seems to be happening, and it is about time some of it reached a wider public domain. Leeds is a place where, historically, street conflict between Left and Right has often been intense, but in the past couple of years, matters have gone from bad to worse. This in itself isn't exceptional, but what gives particular cause for alarm is the possibility that there may be elements connected to the state hyping things up as part of an overall strategy.

For example, in the run up to the April 1993 showing of the *MI5 In Action* C18 documentary, various figures on the Left were rung up by callers *claiming* to be from the League of Saint George, threatening them.[17] This did not happen anywhere else in the country to my knowledge. Furthermore, Bradford (a very short train ride from Leeds) was the place from which virtually all the bogus 'Targetters Targetted' lists, and their variants, (the former certainly produced by MI5/*Searchlight* agent Tim Hepple), were posted out. In June 1993, those individuals in Leeds Anti-Fascist Action responsible for the production of an issue of the Europe-wide *Anti-Fascist Infos*, used it to disseminate outrageous disinformation and lies about myself/Tim Scargill[18]

The November 1993 *MI5 In Action* programme showed a reporter secretly filming a meeting organised by Leeds AFA, and as he entered the room this intrepid character was at pains to point out he had heard about the meeting from someone in *Manchester* — leading me with my suspicious mind to think that the source of the 'information leak' was perhaps much closer to home in Leeds. Additionally, Leeds, and Yorkshire generally, is an area where not only have there been allegations that the BNP (and for a time Third Way) have been 'infiltrated', but little attempt has been made to conceal such penetration. For a start, Leeds AFA's magazine *Attitude* printed a story about Third Way that clearly derived from inside information, and pointed in the direction of a particular person even.[19] As for the BNP, *Searchlight* printed an intriguing story in their August 1994 issue boasting of having obtained a local BNP bulletin *Leeds Patriot* after it had been "left in the pub" (p.6). It defies belief to think that anti-fascists would deliberately admit to covertly monitoring fascist meetings from within the same premises: such would alert Nazi 'counter-intelligence'. This points, therefore, to the state having at least one, or maybe more, operatives inside the local BNP, and them being very confident indeed.[20]

The events surrounding the demise of the *Northern Star* are of national significance. This fine 'alternative' publication, descendant of the *Leeds Other Paper*, was finally forced to shut down (largely as a result of fascist intimidation) in early 1994. The point I find most disturbing is that *C18* magazine featured hundreds of names/personal details from the Leeds and Yorkshire area. Some of those targetted in this way as 'Red Scum' were Labour MPs, and (understandably) they called for the Home Secretary to track down those responsible. The MPs believed that the lists were compiled from "confidential information stolen from the office of a newspaper in Leeds", an obvious reference to the *Northern Star*.[21] That would be reprehensible enough, although not strictly relevant to this essay, but what makes the printing of details from the *Northern Star's* address book in *C18* magazine of great *potential* importance is the disturbing contention that the address book was not stolen at all, but found lying around *in a pub*, exactly what we are meant to believe happened to the July issue of *Leeds Patriot* . . . Now, that may just be local BNP bravado, but if they *did* pick up the address-book that way (or anonymously through the post — like 'Targetters Targetted'), then it would be another highly disturbing thing to have occurred in Leeds. I fully accept that in one of the many fascist incursions into the *Northern Star* office, the address book may have been stolen in the confusion,[22] and this is precisely the account given in the Spring 1994 issue of *Attitude*, produced by Leeds AFA (and others). There, it is stated that "nazi activist Tony White went into the *Northern Star* offices and stole the address book" (p.2). Of interest is the fact that *Attitude* is littered with letters apparently written by another person, then a member of Bradford BNP, boasting about his/their exploits, including the address book theft (p.2). Amazingly, he appears to have written a letter admitting to producing fake (racist) Class War stickers, even down to stating the workplace of a BNP member allegedly involved (p.3). Now, that might simply be accounted for by the fact that many in Bradford BNP have left the party and defected to the British Movement, annoyed by Tyndall's attack on C18, and wanted to 'get back' at the BNP, but it is nevertheless an extraordinary admission. *Attitude* also stated that an attack on SWP paper-sellers 22/1/94 "was co-ordinated on the day by Steve Sargent from London" (p.1), though why there have been no charges laid against him, nor even a photograph shown — that's another question. SWP members have in the past prosecuted fascists for attacks (even if Tim Hepple is immune from prosecution for these and other breaches of the law), so I am at a slight loss to know why charges haven't been brought. I'm not doubting the reality of the attacks in Leeds — just wondering if the identities of the assailants are known for sure.[23]

The writers of *Attitude* obviously work closely with the *Searchlight* 'team', so what they say on any matter has to be treated with great circumspection, unfortunately. Fittingly, they give *Searchlight's* editor a chance to comment that *a propos* Nazi violence, while "in most places the police have been tackling this seriously . . . Yorkshire appears to be a blind spot" (p.2). That may be true — the question is why? When it is recalled that not only has Tony H, the anti-fascist skinhead targetted by both fascists and *Searchlight* spent time in Yorkshire, but the White Wolves document has also circulated there,[24] the cauldron of political intrigue is bubbling nicely — to a recipe concocted elsewhere perhaps. Events in Yorkshire look in part like they are aimed at making the police seem very silly indeed. Referring to the *C18* magazine already analysed above, a letter to Labour MP Max Madden from Assistant Chief Constable Greg Wilkinson said "Those responsible for the publication of the magazine do not wish to be identified and to date our enquiries have not led us to them".[25] Had Wilkinson not read the latest issue of *Attitude?* Or maybe he finds it as reliable and factually accurate as I do — difficult to say. A strong reason for political violence being hyped up in Leeds, and the local police not (necessarily) knowing about it, was evidenced in Madden's response to this rather lame comment by Wilkinson. He called for apprehension of "the people responsible for violence on the far right. If such investigations were handed over to MI5 they might be taken more seriously, although I have no great confidence". This would clearly fit MI5's agenda, and his reluctant endorsement suggests this was an idea impressed upon him by somebody else, close to MI5: very likely *Searchlight*, to whom after all the Leeds AFA leadership defer. A clear way of creating a groundswell of support from Labour MPs for MI5 involvement might well be to use assets to target them (and whole swathes of the Left locally).

Leeds, and Yorkshire generally, is an area where state assets/*agents provocateurs* on the Far Right are no novelty. For example, the 1985 20:20 programme on which Massiter appeared also had a guest slot for one 'Ronnie White', described as an undercover police informant (Special Branch). An exchange with the interviewer went as follows:

(White) "We'd go in force, find a small group of coloureds and hit them with pick-axe handles."

(reporter) "And you were a witness to and participant in all this?"

(White) "Unfortunately, yes."[26]

More recently, Eddie Morrison, who has had a very chequered career in the more violent zones of the fascist fringe felt so aggrieved by allegations that he was a state asset that on 22/8/92 he issued a circular defending himself. This is hardly an impressive document, in my view, containing such nonsense as the suggestion that *Searchlight* might have seen the possibility of libel action against them as a "real threat to their nasty little activities" (p.2). Given that *Searchlight* is a company with no share capital, set up to a large extent with dummy names and addresses, and doesn't even seem to submit accounts, suing it is hardly a realistic option unless one is a millionaire & doesn't mind losing all monies outlaid. I am not saying Morrison is definitely a state asset: merely that he hasn't adequately rebuffed the charge, one made all the more cogent by his long and interesting history, not to mention his close association with 'Agent Hepple' up to and including (according to the latter) co-organising the Dewsbury riot of 1989, which led to the arrests of 82 counter-demonstrators.[27]

The happenings outlined above would point to MI5 (without informing the local Special Branch necessarily) having assets on the Right and, logically, the Left too, the combined (although not for certain individually concerted) effects of which may go some small way towards explaining the turmoil currently occurring there. This statement is not a slur on anti-fascists in Leeds, rather a testimony to their importance that the state should take such a close, interventionist, interest. My raising questions about individuals within Leeds AFA is not personal, it is *political.* I had never written about Leeds before I was attacked in June 1993, although in the light of the above information I can well understand why anyone who was state-connected, whether in Leeds AFA or just feeding information to them to be recycled (*Searchlight*), would feel the need to launch a pre-emptive strike against my credibility. For while I am perfectly willing to accept that the vast majority of Leeds AFA activists and supporters are genuine anti-fascist militants, any of them who are not such, or whose primary allegiance is to the state, would rightly fear someone such as myself drawing together the strands as I have done above. In similar vein, Tyne and Wear Anti-Fascist Association expelled me last year, on the simple grounds that I had *dared* to criticise *Searchlight.* They were so frightened I might defend myself effectively before their membership that they only told me of my expulsion *after* an 'emergency meeting' called to discuss my expulsion: very Kafkaesque. Now, given I had never attended a meeting of TWAFA, I do not regard such an expulsion as *personal* either. They were simply acting in the interests of *Searchlight*/MI5, for whom they are a nice little training-ground. They were not to know at that point that I was fully aware of the TWAFA practice of photographing sellers of the anarchist paper *Class War* on Tyneside in early 1993. Again though, given that photographing anarchists is something that an anti-*fascist* organisation should have no part of, and seems highly likely to have been carried out in the interests of local Special Branch at least (if not MI5), I can well understand the worries of those running TWAFA concerning facts I may have uncovered/may yet uncover in my research. I am sure the memberships of Leeds AFA and TWAFA are in the vast majority unaware of the true significance of the actions undertaken by elements in their leadership, and it was clearly prudence on the part of those elements to get their retaliation in first, so that any facts I reveal about them can be dismissed by reference to my 'personal grievance' or 'vendetta' against them. Unfortunately, in my opinion, the local leadership's actions have only served to heighten my interest in their areas, and in that respect have been counter-productive.

Very recent events in Leeds show the pot there is still on the boil: there have been firebombings of cars, physical attacks on individuals and their homes, in attacks of vicious intensity claimed by people using the label C18 according to the *Guardian* (24/9/94), which recites the familiar litany that "Police . . . inquiries have so far failed to trace members of the group".[28] The *Guardian* did *not* mention recent attacks on BNP members in their homes, including an incident whereby one person had their windows shot through. Now, I am not suggesting that it was MI5 assets who carried out the attacks: local fascists and anti-fascists would seem to be well capable of that without state assistance. What I am saying though, is that there is a possibility that state assets in the ranks of Left *and* Right are active in escalating conflict: the beneficiary of which would be MI5 for certain, in line with their current expansion strategy. Maybe at some point in the future (if they haven't already) MI5 assets will provide arms to both sides. It would certainly aid the definition of fascists and anti-fascists as 'terrorists'.

Is it happening elsewhere?

A reasonable objection to my somewhat sinister interpretation of events in Leeds might be the assertion that things there are unique, and I am reading too much into one case. Perhaps. However I think the pattern is not unique, and would like to draw your attention to events hundreds of miles away over the Scottish border, in Glasgow. This hinges around what I choose to call the 'Missing FiloFax Mystery'. There are a number of different versions, but the basic outline (some parts of which are undoubtedly straightforward) goes like this. In November 1993, a Glasgow Anti-Nazi League member had a personal document stolen by "men in balaclavas". According to Denis

Campbell (no less!) this was a diary,[29], Ken Hyder says it was a filofax,[30] while the coffee-table *Guardian*-style magazine *Red Pepper* says it was both an address book and a diary.[31] Whatever its exact nature, I find it easy to believe some such intimate belonging was stolen, and subsequently SWP members have been harassed by phone messages from people calling themselves C18. Issue 5 of *Target* Spring 1994 featured 60 or so names/addresses, as both Hyder and Campbell point out.

It is at this point that I begin to have some difficulty with the received wisdom, peddled by Campbell, Hyder and *Searchlight*. They ask us to believe that the details used in *Target* came from that theft last November. On perusing the list in *Target* however, things don't quite fit. For a start, for a list supposedly designed to produce phone harassment, it is strange that most individuals listed *do not have phone numbers given*. Especially strange given that (surely?) the purpose of carrying round such details in an address book (or filofax/diary) would primarily be to telephone people? Just as curiously, the names are grouped geographically, by SWP Branch (eg Glasgow East/Glasgow West/Rutherglen etc.). This list then, seems highly likely to have come from a central membership list: not the sort of thing someone would ordinarily write into a diary, even less an address book. For do not people invariably write contacts addresses alphabetically, not the way they are grouped here? If these names and addresses did not, therefore, come in the main from the reported theft, why might some people have an interest in maintaining they did? The answer might be to *cover up* the real source of the information printed in *Target*. Now, I can easily see why *Target* would not be too keen on discussing the sources of information used, in order not to discourage further inflows. Given the absence of key SWP names from the list printed, and lack of reference to highly salient personal details concerning individuals that would be common knowledge to SWP members, it seems to me improbable that fascists infiltrated the SWP to obtain the information, though that is always a possibility. However, what interest could anybody else have in feeding false stories into the public domain concerning this matter, whether by using journalists as witting (or unwitting) dupes? Candidates who might have such an interest are MI5 and Special Branch even, both intent on increasing the level of conflict by facilitating 'hits' by Right on Left, and *vice versa*. This, the passing over to political enemies of membership lists, is, as I have illustrated in *A Lie Too Far* and *At War With The Truth*, a very common *modus operandi* of MI5 assets at this present time. I put some of these points to Mr Hyder in a letter of 21/7/94: to which he chose not to reply — make of that what you will. Maybe there is a simple and innocent answer to the incongruities that puzzle me: in which case, I await one. Meanwhile, I reserve my judgement.

Notes:

1   Including Julie Waterson, ANL spokesperson.

2   For example, see *The Times* 18/10/93 'Police scour video footage in hunt for march infiltrators' by Richard Duce.

3   *The Financial Times, Daily Mail, Evening Standard, Mail on Sunday, Daily Express, Sunday Express, Daily Star, Daily Telegraph* and *Sunday Telegraph* did not oppose the order, readers please note (*Guardian* 27/11/93). *The Sun* handed pictures over voluntarily].

4   *Guardian* 1/12/93. *CARF* criticised the National Union of Journalists, *presumably* (it isn't spelt out) for handing over photographs, and then (laughably) called upon the NUJ to "mount a *political* campaign against journalists becoming an arm of the state" (March/April 1994 p.7). As I hope I am showing, many journalists act as 'arms' of the state now, anyway. An anonymous left-field pamphlet about the march, after discussing the media's supplying photographs, had more direct advice: "hit all the TV cameras, video cameras and photographers. Even if they have fucking Anti-Nazi League stickers on their lapels" (p.9 'Ready, Welling and Able' Pentagon B, Edinburgh 1994).

5   See *Daily Mail* 5/2/94 (Peter Burden), *The Times* 5/2/94 (Stewart Tendler) for example.

6   Written by Gervase Webb and Shekhar Bhatia.

7   See the article 'ANL riot in Welling' in *Combat 18* magazine issue 1 (no page numbers), *Red Action* 67 Spring 1994 p.12 confirms Red Action's presence. *CARF* (November/December 1993 p.13) refers to this clash *and* an earlier attack by C18 on individual demonstrators at Woolwich station. The *Order* (issue 7 Editorial) conflates the Woolwich attack and the events at Abbey Wood, boasting, incorrectly, of the former assault (in which someone apparently lost an eye and another was in a coma) as "another C18 street victory over yellow action".

8   That Duce's *Times* article the same day also mentioned Red Action/Panther confirms they were 'in the frame' — although he didn't mention MI5.

9   See *Panther* Winter 1993/4 issue 9, page 1 — 'Declaration of Independence', and pages 8-9 — 'The Waters Have Parted', a classic *exposé* of 'Militant' manipulation. One reporter alleged (absurdly at best) that the split was between a "section that believed in confrontation and another that did not" (*Independent* 15/11/93, by-line JoJo Moyes).

10 Whose New York (Elridge Cleaver) faction did indeed embark on — some would say were driven to — low level guerilla warfare.

11 Issue 67, p1-12.

12 'Unholy Alliance of Government and Left' *Spearhead* 301 March 1994 p.6-9 (quote is from p.8).

13 *Sigrun* issue 2 December 1933 p.2.

14 *Spearhead* op. cit. p.7. There is another reason Tyndall drew attention to this — to remind doubters upset by his proscription of C18 in December that he has had 'street experience' in the past too.

15 Which is not to say the ANL aren't well capable of circulating *petitions* to demand *the police* storm the telephone box, or selling badges/lollipops/stickers on the same theme, standing behind police lines chanting 'police protect the telephone-boxes', and (most importantly) collecting huge sums of money to employ SWP bureaucrats to call *full-time* for the storming of the telephone box. But actually *do* something themselves — hardly!!.

16 See *Autonome AntiFa* Press Release , *Gottingen* 20/7/94.

17 See for example the report in *Socialist Worker* 27/2/93 p.14.

18 They have so far refused to explain or justify their propagation of these slurs, and it is my contention they have not done so because they *cannot*, which raises the question as to why they circulated them in the first place.

19 Summer 1994 issue 'Small is Beautiful?' It is possible that Leeds AFA didn't know this: indeed their information source may well have been working for the state directly, with them receiving information via a conduit such as *Searchlight*.

20 The plot thickens when *Searchlight* refer to the July 1994 issue of *Leeds Patriot* as having an item on security on page 4. The genuine article has no such item on that page — I do hope somebody hasn't been passing *Searchlight* dummy documents: that would be a role-reversal!.

21 *Yorkshire Evening Post* 14/2/94.

22 See the harrowing account of continual harassment by fascists contained in the article 'Northern Star: Target for racists', *Free Press* (Campaign For Press and Broadcasting Freedom) November 1993 p.7 which graphically indicates the pressure they were under in their final days.

23 Sergant denies a recent "presence in Leeds, Bradford or Grimsby, and haven't been for many years. If you ever come across who ever this person is who is claiming to be me in these areas, I can only presume he is either a red or a cop" *Putsch* 10 March 1994 p.5.

24 See Chapter 'Combat 18 and the state' for details of Tony H and the White Wolves document.

25 *Yorkshire on Sunday* 29/5/94.

26 Transript of US version shown on ABC News Hotline 27/2/85.

27 *At War with Society* (1993) p.16-17.

28 See also report in *Socialist Worker* 3/9/94.

29 *Scotland on Sunday* 24/4/94.

30 *Observer* 22/5/94.

31 October 1994 p.6.

Forging the Loyalist connections

THERE IS NO DOUBT that, in various ways, the activities of Ulster Loyalists are of great interest to MI5. In the Lecture Rimington refers to countering the efforts of the IRA "and those of so-called Loyalist groups — to obtain arms and funds from abroad" (p.8). The banning (in Northern Ireland) of the Ulster Defence Association (UDA) in July 1992 can be seen as evidence of 'serious intent' if that is what is looked for, although the fact this happened after hundreds of UDA murders carried out over 20 years, mostly under the cover-name of the Ulster Freedom Fighters (UFF), casts doubt on the integrity of any intent displayed by the government. This whole area of Ulster Loyalism is a complex one, in which apparently mutually contradictory propositions are advanced by varying commentators. On the one hand, since the 1985 Anglo-Irish Agreement between London and Dublin Loyalists have felt they are being 'squeezed out', ignored by the British government. These feelings have been exacerbated by the December 1993 Downing St Declaration between the two governments, and contemporary revelations that since at least 1989 the British state had (using an MI6 conduit) been talking to the IRA. On the other hand, the Loyalists see themselves as defenders of the status quo, and thereby loyal to the very crown, and government, which (in their view) is planning to off-load them into a united Ireland, or at the least has no serious objection.[1]

The case of Brian Nelson, an MI5 agent who eventually became the 'Intelligence Officer' of the UDA, and in that guise was in charge of compiling files on targets for assassinations, is still one that hasn't been fully told. It became clear at his trial (for setting up two murders) that a lot was suppressed, including his relationship with high-ranking British politicians. The intention of sending Nelson into the UDA was not to 'help' the UDA carry out their own plans, except where they intersected with those of the secret state, and to further 'task' the UDA (unwittingly) with various assassinations the secret state wanted carried out at arms length. This is the real issue: Nelson was being used to 'teleguide' the UDA to wipe out people (such as the solicitor Pat Finucane) the secret state wanted eliminated.[2] That Nelson, an MI5 agent, was jailed for the leaking of files to the UDA, and not one RUC member even charged (as opposed to questioned) might point towards his sacrfice being yet another occasion of inter-agency rivalry between RUC and MI5. On this reading, the banning of the UDA *in Northern Ireland*, just after MI5 took over primacy in such matters concerning England, may have been a strategem, by which the secret state sought to regain the level of influence enjoyed when Nelson was in place, and lost after his removal and the subsequent internal 'purge'. In that situation, the contemporary disinformational 'spin' that MI5 were unhappy with the UDA being banned in Northern Ireland, makes sense. One of the many things Brian Nelson did was to facilitate the January 1988 arms shipment to the UDA/UVF/Ulster Resistance, two thirds of which reached its intended destination[3] and just under half of which is still in Loyalist hands. A report issued by 'Relatives For Justice' in June 1993 gave a list of *sixty three* murders that had been carried out using this weaponry, which had been imported into Northern Ireland under the auspices of MI5.[4] MI5's 'explanation' (if it can be called that) as to how the weapons consignment reached Northern Ireland escaping detection, is that there was a break-down in monitoring procedures![5]

The above facts, and evidently ongoing passing of information by sections of the security forces to Loyalist hit-squads, leads many, especially Republicans, to see the Loyalists as a mere appendage of the British state. I do not think this is so however, theirs is a complex relationship of both dependency *and* rebellion. The 450 Loyalists incarcerated in Northern Ireland jails are testimony to the fact that there is no exact simultaneity of interest, contrasting (for example) with the fact that virtually no Right-wing murderers of Leftists were imprisoned in the Weimar Republic, or the more recent impunity with which state-sponsored death squads operate in various South American countries. I have yet to see any rebuttal of Bruce's claim that, comparing convictions to actions undertaken, the 'security forces' have "greater success . . . in apprehending Loyalist Killers".[6] This fact does not *negate* evidence of intermittent collusion on various levels, at various times, but it certainly has to be placed alongside it. On the political level, it is unquestionable that Loyalist intransigents have been frozen out, especially since 1985. The reaction in Loyalist paramilitary circles to the Nelson case was to move in on other agents/suspected agents, and clear them out, one way or another. The upsurge in Loyalist military activity, while undoubtedly using much of the weaponry supplied courtesy of MI5, has nonetheless been undertaken as a means of distancing themselves from the current 'peace process'. However much this may seem to coincide with MI5's agenda, the paramilitaries have their own reasons for acting this way, that are definitely not imposed from the outside. Loyalist beliefs and aspirations won't 'disappear' if the British troops withdraw, and the sooner all outside commentators understand this the better. Unquestionably, Loyalist paramilitaries are far more amenable to MI5/RUC infiltration/surveillance than Republicans. This is due to reasons of ideology, residential location and composition of the RUC (a non-Catholic force), and the longer history of 'self-reliance' exhibited by the IRA throughout the 20th Century against many foes.[7]

MI5's ultimate intentions in Northern Ireland, as regards both Loyalists and Republicans, are difficult to be certain about. But, there a number of parameters to go on. Firstly, going right back to the 1970's, the last thing MI5 wants is a 'peaceful settlement', for that would be an erosion of their capacity for autonomous action and the untrammelled exercise of power, including murder. Thus the IRA 'ceasefire' announced at the end of August 1994 will have set them severe long-term problems potentially. Secondly, any operations they undertake in Ireland are done so for their own reasons, having only a tangential superficial relation to government agendas and the desire to 'fight terrorism'. Thirdly, the RUC Special Branch, who at present have operational primacy in Northern Ireland when it comes to 'anti-terrorism' are seen as rivals, to be excluded and tricked at every opportunity. Neither tells each other any more than they are forced to about operations/agents, and the feeling of dislike is mutual. Fourthly, in the light of the foregoing, it seems increasingly likely that MI5 will both mount operations against *and* seek to manipulate Loyalists for their own ends, while retaining ultimate contempt for them and their beliefs. The Loyalists have weaponry (if as yet not a huge amount of explosives), a youthful command-cadre who are increasingly technically proficient, and are feeling more and more bitter about betrayal (as they see it) by the British government. The overall political climate is volatile, making a situation ripe for intrigue — just how MI5 like it.

It has often been remarked that Northern Ireland is a 'laboratory' in which political/military techniques are perfected, and then used in Britain. This is so today, but it is my contention that the traffic is two-way: concerns that have hitherto been primarily seen as ones outside Northern Ireland, and not originating there, have been imported, because they fit the agenda of the secret state. This applies to a desire to hype up Nazi-Loyalist links, and if possible use them to facilitate operations in England itself, as a prelude and accompaniment to further repressive legislation going beyond the confines of Northern Ireland. A spreading of Loyalist paramilitary activity to England (for whatever reason) would help MI5 consolidate their profile. The albeit arrogant and supercilious view of Rupert Allason MP, who is close to their long-time rival, MI6, illustrates the level of intra-state hostility faced by Rimington & her crew. He pointed out that "while the Provisionals and Loyalists pose a threat to themselves and their rivals in Ulster, they do not undermine our parliamentary democracy. More British soldiers die each year on German autobahns than are killed in terrorist attacks. Does MI5 really have to be involved at all?"[8]

A Polish mazurka: the Loyalist arms shipment stunt

While others have well-ploughed this furrow, mention must be made here of a major MI5 operation, intimately involving Rimington personally, that surfaced in late 1993.[9] On 24th November, a captured arms cache originating in Poland and destined for Northern Ireland, a joint UFF/UVF enterprise (the UVF being dominant), was revealed to a suitably impressed media at Teesport docks, Cleveland. The haul was extensive: 320 AKM assault rifles (updated Kalashnikovs): 60,000 rounds of ammu-nition: 50 Makarov pistols: 500 hand grenades, and (in the informed words of Keith Dovkants "most significant of all, two tons of commercial grade plastic explosive with hundreds of detonators".[10] The interception of such looked at first like a major MI5 (and/or MI6 — there was some confusion) coup, and testament to their willingness to crack down on Loyalists.

As time went by, however, it transpired that this was a classic 'sting' operation, in which the whole enterprise had been set up by MI5 from start to finish, in collusion with the Polish 'State Protection Office' (ie secret service): UOP, eager as the latter is to ingratiate themselves with Western Europeans now the Cold War is over, and whose government harbours aspirations (and has lodged applications) to become a full member of both NATO and the EC. Worrying questions began to surface: in particular, if this was an anti-Loyalist operation pure and simple, why were the arms not traced back to Northern Ireland, and those picking them up/distributing them trailed and apprehended? The absence of arrests, and the contrived nature of the affair led some, such as *An Phoblacht/Republican News* to see it as a "badly formulated publicity stunt" (9/12/93): Robin Ramsay was (as usual) closer to the mark when he described it as a rather successful 'psychological-operation' (the term used to apply to state-sponsored massaging of the public mind to further propaganda aims).[11] While questions had been posed earlier, for instance the *Guardian* reported an offer by the new UOP head to resign, because stings are illegal in Poland (2/12/93), it was Dovkants' *Evening Standard* article of 22/12 that really caused the fur to fly, coinciding as it did with the *Scotsman* article on Loyalists of 17/12 mentioned earlier. The *Standard* piece led directly to a 'D' notice being imposed.[12] The story took a month to resurface. which it duly did in the (Dublin) *Irish Press* 28/1/94, quoting a Polish secret state source as admitting the operation was a sting, thus confirming what Dovkants had written.

So: why did MI5 undertake the endeavour, and why has news of it been allowed to percolate into the public domain? A wide range of motivations for the scam have been put forward, all deserving consideration. They are as follows, and remember none are mutually exclusive:

1   A propaganda exercise, designed, just before the Downing Street declaration, as a "political and psychological operation" to influence the Dublin government into accelerating the 'peace process' by alerting them to the reality of potential Loyalist military might (The UOP position),[13] a viewpoint not contradicted by a Polish government spokesperson — or confirmed for that matter.[14] If this was so, I don't see why Loyalists weren't allowed to take delivery of the weapons anyway: that would make the point even more forcefully.[15] Furthermore, the initiative for such is unlikely to have emanated from the government: rather too clever for John Major. So, a possibility ranking of 4.5/10.

2   To deter illegal arms dealers from coming to Poland, another UOP position (*Guardian* 2/12/93, *Evening Standard* 22/12/93). This might conceivably explain the Polish rationale, but not MI5's. I don't think it totally holds water even from

the declared Polish viewpoint: it certainly advertised Poland/Eastern Europe generally, as a source of arms. But, a definite factor, earning a mark of 7.5/10.

3   A propaganda stunt to coincide with publication of the 'Intelligence Services Bill', putting MI6 on a statutory footing for the first time (*Lobster* 27 p.16). A good explanation as regards *timing*, but too fanciful as regards origin and gestation, particularly in light of the subsequent *demise* of Pauline Neville-Jones, on which more below. 7/10.

4   A diversion, as a result of which the UVF was able "to smuggle in another shipment three weeks earlier" (*Evening Standard* 22/12/93). A very disturbing possibility, which (as the 1988 shipment showed) wouldn't be without precedent. However, while Loyalists seem to have acquired commercial explosives, there is as yet little evidence of the UVF in particular upgrading their level of armaments overall in recent months. For the moment, this claim can be marked down as RUC-inspired disinformation. 3.5/10.

5   Something designed to harm Loyalists. This has some merit, for despite the lack of arrests, the cash reputedly paid out (and still unaccounted for), £250,000, would have been a significant amount to them. It would have the merit of forcing Loyalists to look further afield for finance: both within Northern Ireland and elsewhere, making such extraordinary and urgent efforts easier to trace than normal contacts would be. In this sense, the operation would act as an 'orange dye', highlighting connections between Loyalists in Ulster and elsewhere. The only slight problem with this thesis is the figure of £250,000: far too high for the merchandise eventually captured, which would have a maximium price of about £80,000. Logically, this might point to some arms having got through (explanation 4), but there is little hard evidence.[16] 7.5/10

6   Squeezing Loyalist finances would also have the potential effect of driving them, logistics-wise, into the political arms of those (like UK Fascists but also English/Scottish/Welsh sympathisers generally) from whom the paramilitaries have for reasons of security chosen to keep a healthy distance. The operation showed exactly what it is that the Loyalists want, in terms of hard-ware, creating a 'space' for state-sponsored *agents provocateurs* to mingle with genuine sympathisers, hawking their wares (just as was mentioned above for Scotland). Again, quite plausible: 8/10

7   An endeavour intended to push the UDA/UVF into criminality of a non-political kind, resulting in a corrosion of their organisational morale and a decline in popular support. Two observations must be made here. First, reports of Loyalist (and Republican) 'criminality' have often been fiction, and such as there is on both sides has been exaggerated out of all proportion, in the interests of disinformation. Partly, it's a question of definition: what Dovkants describes as "extortion", eg revenue from Protestant 'black taxis' and small businesses, is seen by the paramilitaries (and no doubt the donors) as merely unofficial community-based

taxation, albeit unpopular at times. To simply see this as racketeering (whether in Loyalist *or* Republican areas) is to misconstrue the degree of popular legitimacy and mass base *both* sets of paramilitaries have. The accounting for/use of money *once collected* is a slightly different matter, and we shouldn't analytically blur the two, even if it has been the Loyalist paramilitary leadership rather more than Republicans who have sometimes tended to be 'light-fingered'. Secondly, the attempt to portray fund-raising efforts by the 'mainland'-based Loyalist Prisoners Aid and suchlike as 'criminal' is even more questionable. Those two things said, the *aspiration* on the part of MI5 is certainly quite feasible. 7/10.

8   To enhance MI5's profile, and 'put one over' the RUC, as part of an ongoing struggle by MI5 to take over the intelligence-gathering lead in Northern Ireland itself, a point made by Kevin McNamara, Labour's Shadow Northern Ireland Secretary (*Belfast Telegraph* 28/1/94). This seems highly likely to me, and doesn't conflict with the other possibilities above. The *Evening Standard* article of 22/12 bore all the hallmarks of an RUC propaganda counter-strike, and as we shall see later, the RUC Chief Constable Hugh Annesley (despite public mellifluousness) has a definite, personal, game-plan by which he hopes to outmaneouvre MI5, and to an extent even RUC Special Branch, in the *Dirty War* between the two agencies. 9/10.

As to why news of the 'Polish *Mazurka*' has filtered through, part of it is because by its very nature it was a 'media event', thus *some* journalists were bound to ask a few questions. Then there is the aforementioned RUC SB-MI5 rivalry: no way was this ploy going to go unchallenged. Furthermore, the UOP and the Polish government too were involved, and the very reasons for participating in the operation from their point of view meant a second post-November, dose of accredited publicity would do them no harm at all. Upsetting MI5 slightly wouldn't matter, because not only has all not come out, MI6 would have been egging the UOP on to do precisely that: embarrass MI5.

The minute questions were asked, not least by the Cabinet, it is obvious somebody's head would have to roll. The one that did was that of Pauline Neville-Jones, Chair of the 'Joint Intelligence Committee' (JIC). This is very understandable: the JIC is the body that supposedly co-ordinates the activities of MI5, MI6, GCHQ, the MOD and Treasury, providing weekly reports to the PM. The JIC has a broad remit, relevantly including "liaison with . . . foreign intelligence organisations" and to "bring to the attention of Ministers and Departments . . . assessments that appear to require operational, planning or policy action".[17] The JIC Chair "is "responsible for the broad supervision of the work of the JIC. He (*sic*) is specifically charged with ensuring that the Committee's warning and monitoring role is discharged effectively. He has direct access to the Prime Minister".[18] This is what a document published in September 1993, with a foreword by Major, said. Even accounting for our charismatic Prime

Minister's extremely fickle memory, which allegedly saw him suffer total memory loss about documents he signed as Chancellor/Foreign Secretary concerning arms to Iraq, trouble for which the JIC could reasonably be blamed was just around the corner. So, when the excrement began to publicly hit the air-conditioning in December, Neville-Jones was sacrificed, being moved sideways (ie demoted) to a Foreign Office sinecure.

It has since come out, though not in the British press, that a prime candidate for the chop in this affair should have been Rimington herself. For contrary to earlier reports which had put Neville-Jones in the frame as having visited Warsaw in November 1993, to finalise timings and reassure a jittery UOP, the functionary visiting was Stella Rimington.[19] That she was able to make Neville-Jones carry the can is an ample demonstration of Rimington's skill at avoiding personal trouble, as well as a wonderful proof that MI5 have few constraints on them even within the state apparatus itself. If the 'nominal superior' is sacked for an action carried out autonomously by a supposed subordinate agency (MI5), then anything goes. The dexterity with which Rimington evaded responsibility has been matched by her subsequent cheek. For, knowing full well the still-operative 'D' notice would prevent the tame media from commenting adversely, she had the following to say in the Lecture, which you are now in possession of enough information to fully savour, bland as it appears. She said "Last year . . . a joint operation involving a number of agencies halted a large consignment of weapons originating in Poland and destined for so-called Loyalist terrorists in Northern Ireland" (p.5): what a multitude of intrigue does that sentence conceal, and who in the media has dared contrast this with the reality, or will? Nobody.

How does this saga fit into the parameters of MI5-Loyalist relations sketched in above? Quite well, actually. It's all there: heavy MI5 infiltration of the same, as well as ripping them off, pushing them in directions they may not want to go. The lack of arrests might provide ideological ammunition to those who want to see in it evidence of Loyalist-state collaboration, should they so wish. However, MI5 is less interested in arrests than being able to influence operations. In this respect, arresting *no-one* in the UDA/UVF only heightens internal paramilitary unease, as they search for a high-level agent (or agents) without even the clues selective arrests might have brought. Unhindered as they are by the inconvenience of legality, more of the same is on the way from MI5, indeed another instalment may already have arrived, as we shall see below.

Notes:

1 For acute insights into the current Loyalist mind see the works of Steve Bruce *The Red Hand* (on paramilitaries/1992) and *On The Edge of the Union* (on current political ideology/1994) — both published by Oxford University Press. The only two other recent books on Loyalist political thinking are Arthur Aughey *Under Siege: Ulster Unionism and the Anglo-Irish Agreement* (Blackstaff Press, Belfast 1989) and Sarah Nelson *Ulster's*

Uncertain Defenders (Appletree Press, Belfast 1984). A rather different, and more critical, view of Loyalism can be found in Michael Farrell's classic *Northern Ireland: The Orange State* (Pluto Press, London 1980).

2   Dorril *op. cit.* p.198-203 is a reasonable summary, with references. More typical is the sparse treatment in Mark Urban's *Big Boys Rules* (Faber & Faber 1992) which merely comments that the "case raised disturbing questions about the security forces' responses to foreknowledge of Republican and Loyalist attacks" (p.217), but even this vapidity is trumped by Bruce's comment that "Nelson was a UDA man helping the security forces rather than the other way round. His information allowed a large number of UDA plans to be subverted while the UDA gained nothing in return" (*Red Hand* p.264). Understandably, this is a sore (blind) spot for someone as sympathetic to Loyalism as Bruce, but as I've said, Nelson *infiltrated* the UDA on the secret state's behalf, not *vice versa*. Hints of his activities came out in press reports: see the *Independent* 9/1/92, 23/1/92, 30/1/92, 4/2/92 & 9/6/92, the *Guardian* 23/1/92, 30/1/92 and 4/2/92, *Sunday Times* 26/1/92, and Paul Foot in the *Daily Mirror* 1/2/92. Also see the postcript 'Terrorist Agents' in Martin Dillon's *Stone Cold* Hutchinson 1992 p.229-234, and *Irish News* 11/1/92, 23/1/92, 30/1/92, 4/2/92, plus the summary in *Statewatch* March-April 1992 p.4-5.

3   For an outline see 'Arms To Loyalists' in the 1993 Wolfe Tone programme commemorating the deaths of James Connolly/Bobby Sands. A common misconception is that the arms were 'South African': rather they came from the Lebanon, via an introduction (and possibly finance) *provided by* BOSS.

4   *Shoot To Kill and Collusion* (Relatives For Justice Mervue, Galway June 1993). See also the recent Amnesty report *Political Killings in Northern Ireland* which analyses deaths caused by *all* sides — paramilitaries *and* the state. They too raise similar disturbing questions about collusion, as did former MI6 operative Fred Holroyd in *War Without Honour* (with Nick Burbridge) Medium, Hull 1989. Attempts to deny the significance of the information imparted by Holroyd/Wallace started in a big way with a major piece by David McKittrick (that *doyenne* of disinformers) in the *Independent* 2/9/87, wherein he used the general credibility he had accumulated (even publishing some of Wallace's earlier material on the 'Wilson Plot') to comprehensively savage Holroyd/Wallace, with the *Independent* not allowing them 'right of reply'. The standard book-form defence against the collusion charge is to be found in Martin Dillon *The Dirty War* (Arrow 1991 p.189-97), and see also Urban *op. cit.* ch. 5 as well as Bruce *The Red Hand* p.199-214. The counter-attack on those who deny the veracity of Wallace/Holroyd's allegations is contained in Robin Ramsay's *Colin Wallace — an assessment* (*Lobster* 14 1987 p.17-25), as well as his *Smearing Wallace & Holroyd* (*Lobster* 15 1988 p.8-12). Also of interest is Ken Livingstone MP's 'maiden speech' to the Commons (7/7/87) outlining the key allegations (reprinted in *Lobster* 14 p.26-9), Paul Foot's rebuttal of McKittrick in *Who Framed Colin Wallace* (p.366-86), and the review of Dillon's *Dirty War* in *Lobster* 21 May 1991 p.26. Finally, I would remind disinformers everywhere that if you can't stick to the truth you should at least tell consistent lies: Dillon's *Dirty War* says that Kenneth Littlejohn (a 1970's *agent provocateur*/MI6 agent) was not, when acting illegally, robbing banks for example, doing so on behalf of the secret state (p.102/106). Two years later, in *Stone Cold*, Dillon casually refers to the Littlejohn brothers as having been "encouraged

to become involved in terrorist activity" (p.231). A new script-writer is called for: maybe Dillon should approach that willing vehicle of disinformation the BBC series 'Between The Lines'. . .

5   *Inside Ulster* (BBC) 28/1/93.
6   *The Red Hand* p.298.
7   See the explanation of the relative ease with which Loyalists are penetrated by the MI5 source in Dillon *Stone Cold* p.161-2.
8   *Independent* 14/6/94.
9   Sources are detailed in *Statewatch* January-February 1994 'MI5/MI6 — Trick or Treat?' (p.7-8) and Robin Ramsay *The Great Polish Arms Find Caper Lobster* 27, June 1994 p.16.
10   *Evening Standard* 22/12/93.
11   *Lobster* 27, June 1994 p.16.
12   *Intelligence Newsletter* 7/4/94 p.7.
13   *Irish Press* 28/1/94.
14   *Irish Times* 29/1/94.
15   They were addressed to Freckleton's, a well-known building supply company in Belfast (*Irish Times* 2/12/93).
16   One reason for exaggerating the amount of cash laid out might have been to underline growing middle-class/professional (and hence well-heeled) support for the paramilitaries.
17   *Central Intelligence Machinery* (HMSO September 1993) p.23-24.
18   *Op. cit.* p.11.
19   *Intelligence Newsletter* 7/4/94 p.6-7.

Hitler & William of Orange: united in struggle?

AT THE SAME TIME as the Left was being linked with the IRA/INLA, another propaganda campaign played up links between fascists (in particular 'Combat 18') and Loyalist paramilitaries. This reached a peak in the *MI5 In Action* TV documentary shown 19/4/93, which was ostensibly on Combat 18. I say ostensibly, because when two alleged members of C18, Charlie Sergeant and Eddie Whicker, were questioned on screen by our old friend Andrew Bell (on whom more below), especially in Whicker's case, it wasn't primarily about C18, but Ulster Loyalism.[1] Further doubt is cast on the veracity of the programme because the key 'witness' of such links, 'Simon', is someone highly unlikely to have been in possession of much confidential knowledge concerning such matters.[2] The UDA took a dim view (as might be expected) of the 'documentary', making the interesting (if slightly flawed) point that had Whicker and Sergeant actually been members of a "Loyalist paramilitary grouping" then by "allowing these two men to be heard Granada (were) either in breach of the law, or implicitly saying that their overt claims of paramilitary membership were lies".[3]

'Two pints and a revolver please': the English UDA

Following the *MI5 in Action* programme, Eddie Whicker (ex-NF and a prominent UK distributor of UDA literature) and Frank Portinari (reputed to be Commander of the London UDA) as well as James McCrudden (a well-known Belfast Loyalist & ex-UDR member) were arrested on gun-running charges. Whicker was released without charge, and when the case came to full trial an intriguing pattern of events emerged, which may well fit into the overall picture of MI5 strategy far more than it appears to at first sight.

To rehearse the basic facts of the case, on 31/5/93 Portinari (a London-born Irish Catholic who had been in and out of fascist groups like the NF and BNP throughout the 1980's) was apprehended in the car park of the Crown & Cushion pub in Perry Bar, Birmingham, transferring some weapons and ammunition to McCrudden's car. The weapons themselves, seven hand-guns, some of which were vintage items, were hardly the most up to date models, certainly not the AK47s laughably claimed by one source.[4] Portinari claimed he had bought the weapons under duress, from various pubs in East and South London, after having been threatened by UDA heavies in an Ulster drinking club. Perhaps, but it seems far more likely that these weapons were from the London UDA store, and he was transferring them to the Midlands for security reasons — ironically enough following the *MI5 In Action* programme heavily stressing such links, in line with MI5's agenda to accentuate them.[5] When the case came to trial, Portinari received a 5 year sentence, McCrudden 2.5 years.

It is the manner of the men's apprehension, the sentencing, and the sparse media attention the case received, that are its most interesting aspects, because they highlight yet again inter-agency rivalry between MI5 and Special Branch, and in the course of doing so raise further questions. To deal with the apprehension of the men, according to a most detailed article in the *Mail on Sunday* co-written by Jay Rayner and Denis Campbell, hereafter 'Raynbell'.[6] Denis Campbell, sometime staff writer on the London weekly *Time Out*, and author of the Scottish piece analysed earlier, is a long-time associate, like the producer of the *MI5 In Action* special on C18 Andrew Bell, of *Searchlight* magazine, which in my estimation makes *both* of them 'MI5 errand-boys', an impression only strengthened by the content of both the programme and the article, especially as the latter draws on the former, right down to quoting 'Simon' extensively,[7] Eddie Whicker was trailed by "Special Branch officers and intelligence service personnel" to Birmingham, carrying the same holdall later used by Portinari to transport the weapons.[8] It is my understanding that Whicker contends he used the holdall for moving the Ulster Loyalist magazines he sells, and in any event his fingerprints were found on the outside of the bag, but not inside, nor on the weapons.[9] Raynbell affect to find it highly sinister that charges against Whicker "were dropped because, in the absence of any search of the holdall at the time, they had no evidence it contained the guns".[10] On reflection, this assertion is either just stupid — or more sinister on their part. For, if Whicker *did* have the weapons in the holdall, he would hardly be likely to carry them to Birmingham himself, and then *bring them back* to London, to then give them to Portinari — who would transport them back to Birmingham again!! If the absurdity of this sinks in, then Raynbell's next assertion is equally bizarre — them finding it "peculiar . . . that it seems the police at no time had any intention of stopping Whicker while they tailed him".[11] In the absence of any indication Whicker had done anything illegal, there is no reason why they should have pulled him up — indeed to have done so would have compromised the later trailing of Portinari. Raynbell go on to take a further swipe at Special Branch, criticising their failure to request extensive local back up for the "surveillance operation on Whicker", in contrast to that on Portinari two days later. What they miss out is the fact that it is highly likely, indeed virtually certain, that the reason there was no extensive surveil-lance on Whicker is that the forces of the state *knew* where the arms were, and that it was Portinari, not Whicker, who would transport them. Which raises the question, why concentrate on Whicker's role? The answer, it seems to me, is to encourage

Loyalists to, between the lines, finger him as a state asset, an impression no doubt intended to be reinforced by him not being charged.

A subsidiary theme of the *Mail on Sunday* article is the implication that Portinari (and maybe McCrudden too) acted as a grass, and in return received a relatively light sentence — "the only likely explanation".[12] And there is no getting away from it — if you contrast the sentences given to Heffernan/McMonagle for attempting to steal what were alleged to be inert explosives with those for Portinari/McCrudden, there is a great disparity, as too with the differing media profiles. Some of the assertions in the article are just garbage — for instance, past membership of the NF/BNP, and selling Loyalist propaganda as well being involved in the UDA *on the mainland* are at present entirely legal activities, and hardly worthy, *on their own*, as such, of the sinister construction put upon them by Raynbell.[13] There are two highly pertinent questions which Raynbell must answer — just why do they think the state gave them extensive access to Portinari's personal effects, including photographs? Might it not be because by means of their article the authors were running errands for the state — 'the only likely explanation'? What wasn't mentioned to *Mail on Sunday* readers was the fact that this whole operation would have been under MI5 control — not that of Special Branch, who like the prosecution are heavily criticised, while MI5 are not even named. It may be that Portinari (and Whicker) *did* roll over and provide information — in which case, why have there not been yet more arrests, other than the one mentioned below, which is apparently unconnected? An equally (if not more) likely scenario than that of Portinari/Whicker as 'grasses' is the possibility these two are being offered as scapegoats to divert attention from MI5/SBs real assets. This scenario may have been in the minds of the UDA's *New Ulster Defender* in April, when they commented on the case. After obtaining an admission from Rayner that he acquired photos used in the article from the police, mainland correspondent 'Charles Black' "put the question to Jay Rayner bluntly. Was he printing disinformation about a Loyalist on behalf of the security services in return for photographs, information and other assistance in writing the article. He refused to be drawn, merely saying that he stood by the article, contradictions and all. Readers of the *New Ulster Defender* can draw their own conclusions".[14] This is a highly disturbing allegation, and I wrote to Rayner to clarify the situation. He denied that MI5 had helped in the preparation of the article, so at first sight was putting across a different line than he had allowed *New Ulster Defender* to imply when he spoke to them. Rayner went on, however, to say that he is "not willing to confirm or deny anything about anybody who helped me with the piece".[15] In which case, why should we take seriously his denial it was MI5? There is a strong balance of probability he is using this form of words to allow him to avoid admitting he has knowingly used as sources MI5 conduits: a term that I believe applies to both *Searchlight* and Denis Campbell, though obviously not exclusively them. The involvement of Denis Campbell/*Searchlight* with the article's production was something *New Ulster Defender* didn't pick up on — but English Nazi circles did. An editorial in *The*

Order issue 7 said that since Portinari's "sentence the left wing including certain sunday newspapers have tried to smear Frank's good name, using lies fed them by *Searchlight's* staff". This, to my mind, is confusing an MI5 *conduit, Searchlight,* with the agency itself. The very idea that the *Mail on Sunday* is 'left-wing' indicates a poverty of political understanding. The newspaper did not print the story, nor *Searchlight* feed it to them, because of any Left-Right reason, but because it suited the interests of the (secret) state.[16]

Explaining the actions of Raynbell is one thing, but of more salience is the operation itself, the precise motives are difficult to pin down, but there are some useful pointers available. For a start, the low level of armaments being transported indicates the English branch of Ulster Loyalism has at present little technological capacity. Further, the panic removal of arms from London seems to illustrate mainland Loyalists were in a *defensive* phase, not preparing to mount an offensive. The purpose of the exercise may well have been to 'take out' both Portinari and (by suspicion) Whicker from English UDA circles, in order to make way for others more congenial to the interests of the state. There is one interpretation of the Portinari case that would make it more straightforward than I have speculated: assuming Portinari *did* buy the weapons in the pubs he suggested, members of the 'criminal fraternity', having just sold weapons to him, might then have run off and told their local police that they had just sold weapons for use in 'terrorist' activity — thereby ensuring they received a second payment, for information about the destination. Very possible, however a problem with that explanation is the media coverage just dissected. Information wasn't imparted to Raynbell for no reason: there was a definite anti-Special Branch/pro-MI5 agenda in operation. That of itself wouldn't totally preclude Portinari having grassed: MI5 are quite capable of using their conduits to 'blow' Special Branch assets as part of their ongoing warfare. On present evidence though, Portinari should be given the benefit of the doubt.

As to whether the source of information on the arms transfer was an MI5 asset, an SB one, a 'common criminal' or just the result of plain communications interception — we'll have to wait and see. The truth, should it ever emerge, is likely to take a long time coming, especially as a whole series of *agent provocateur* entrapment operations concerning English Loyalist sympathisers are going on up and down the country, to a virtual news black-out. Partly, these cases may be MI5 reaping the benefits of the Polish Mazurka: pushing the UDA into reliance on arms sources they'd normally prefer not to be associated with. One of the most important cases to receive the 'silent treatment', not reported in any paper I have yet come across, was that arising out of the arrest in December 1993 of Terry Blackham. At one time Blackham was a prominent NF member, both helping out in administration at NF HQ, and acting as Chairman Ian Anderson's personal bodyguard. He had of late become disillusioned with the NF, and drifted away towards Glasgow Loyalist circles. According to Ian Anderson, Blackham dropped out of the NF after the 1992 General Election, which would strongly indicate the following crime wasn't exactly carrying out party policy.[17] Blackham's arrest came after he was trailed by London Special Branch, first to Birmingham and later to Dumfries in Scotland, where he was apprehended carrying some hand-guns and a rocket-launcher.[18] He received a four year jail sentence, and pleaded guilty, on 17/3/94. His removal from the political scene obviously has ramifications in terms of fascist-Loyalist associations, and also raises an interesting analytical conundrum. It isn't easy to tell the difference between someone arrested because of straightforward detection, and somebody targetted by the state for removal for political reasons, and either fitted up or drawn in as the result of *agent provocateur* activities. It is this very difficulty of course, along with media disinterest (or disinformation), that makes it difficult for outsiders to discern what is significant and what is coincidence. The lack of media interest in the Blackham case may well point to a 'D' notice, as too could the silence so far concerning the Northampton trial, concluded 17/8/94, of four English UDA members, arrested in possession of arms and ammunition on the M6, with two men (Logan and Johnston) receiving sentences of 2.5 and 8 years respectively. It is not yet clear if there was another Far Right connection here, but in the cases of Portinari and Blackham, the link is clear.

What is unusual about the Portinari and Blackham cases, and fully consonant with MI5's current agenda, is the linkage of UK fascists in an *operational* sense with Ulster Loyalists, even if it is only an indirect, logistical link, concerning arms (in Portinari's case transferring them within England), in Blackham's case, presumably, taking them over to Northern Ireland. The UDA has in recent times, as we've seen, mounted an extensive campaign to rearm itself — as instanced in the two arms seizures on Merseyside so far in 1994, which led one newspaper to suggest that "Merseyside Loyalists may have an intelligence services mole within their ranks".[19] So far though, all these episodes point to is the traditional 'sympathiser' role of taking weapons to Northern Ireland. Is there anything else in the offing? That is the big question.

Notes:

1 I understand that the far right first heard about the programme when John Nicholson, of the English UDA, was offered money to appear to spout a pre-ordained script concerning alleged connections between fascists and the UDA. He is said (perhaps implausibly) to have not even been aware of who some of the fascists actually were, and didn't play ball.

2 Careful readers will note I have now revised my view as to the total non-existence of 'Simon' as expressed in *A Lie Too Far* (footnote 6 p.20). Nonetheless, much of what was attributed to him was fictional. He has now disappeared from the fray, having 'found Jesus', and good luck to him.

3 *New Ulster Defender* July 1993 p.10.

4 South London AFA Bulletin November 1993 p.4.

5 For once I am in agreement here with *Searchlight* (March 1994 p.5). That said, if (for

once) they are telling the truth, there has to be a devious reason: most probably to make more believable the other disinformation being passed by themselves and Rayner/Bell.

6   Published in the review 27/2/94 p.41-43.

7   I use the term 'errand-boy' to be not only precise but deliberately insulting: given the first of countless attacks on myself by *Searchlight* baselessly accused me of desiring to be a fascist 'errand-boy' (July 1992 p.10).

8   p.42.

9   Making somewhat disingenuous the *Searchlight* comment that he "had handled the packages containing the guns" (March 1994 p.5).

10   p.43.

11   p.43.

12   p.43 backed up by *Searchlight* March 1994 p.5.

13   And of course *Searchlight* itself, see March 1994 p.5 for more on the same lines. *Time Out* (in an article *not* written by Campbell) took a rather more sympathetic view of Portinari's plight — see 'Babes and Arms' 16/2/94 p.14.

14   Volume 1 no. 9 April 1994.

15   Letter to author 3/6/94.

16   Illustrating yet again the value of *Searchlight* to MI5 as a 'lightning conductor', diverting the attention of target audiences.

17   Letter to author in response to query about Blackham, July 1994.

18   Dumfries is a traditional resting-point before reaching Stranraer, the point of embarkation to Northern Ireland.

19   See the *Irish Post* 26/2/94 'Fears Grow of Loyalist arms stockpile on Merseyside'.

The Fascist spectre — another demon to conjure with

MI5 INTEREST IN the far left hasn't precluded a close, and potentially quite similar (and ambitious) interest in fascists. This should be no surprise: in both MI5 and Special Branch, the same sub-sections investigate the far right and far left. As well as providing a sop to liberal opinion, repressive measures used first against the Right can then be more easily used against the Left (Anti-Nazi League please note), as the brochure makes clear, singling out right-wing groups for a special mention. We are informed that MI5 "monitors the possibility of extreme right-wing, nationalist and racist groups on the Continent establishing contact with sympathisers in this country" (p.17). Since this has already happened (the Euro-Ring, yearly trips to Dixmuide for the festival and to Germany for the Rudolf Hess march, the Blood & Honour network etc.), the passage is cheap rhetoric. In the Dimbleby Lecture, Rimington reiterated MI5's interest in "groups on the extreme right who are seeking to undermine democracy through the exploitation of racial hatred and xenophobia" (p.6-7). John Tyndall, presumably just mishearing the lecture, later wrote that she had said MI5's "focus had changed, from Communist groups to the extreme Right".[1] This was not what she said, so his subsequent comments about Left vs Right thereby fall.

When considering fascist-state relations, it must be borne in mind not all on the far right are antagonistic to the state. *League Sentinel*, journal of the Nazi umbrella-group the League of Saint George pointed out in May 1993, *a propos* the IRA, that they had "made available copies of . . . extensive files on those Marxist and Anti-Fascist Groups who are most likely to be giving the bombers assistance and comfort, to both Special Branch and MI5, and we wish them 'Good Hunting'".[2] The BNP have been careful to distinguish between the police and the government, for example in speaking of successful legal action by BNP supporters against the Metropolitan police *British Nationalist* "stressed that the legal action was not against the police, whom we support, but rather against the government".[3] General attitudes towards the state aside, the one part of fascist activism that has definitely come in for some hype recently has been the activities of the spectral 'Combat 18' (C18), to which I shall now turn.

Combat 18 — new Nazis on the block

I will not dwell on C18 any more than necessary, only looking at it to the extent necessary to draw out pertinent aspects. The prominence given to C18 in both media and Left mythology means that they need to be examined in rather more detail than they might have been otherwise. A key problem encountered in writing about C18 is the plethora of disinformation, emanating both from the Far Right *and* state-connected sources. Fascists themselves have engaged in subterfuge to cover their tracks, making prosecutions for illegal incitement/conspiracy more difficult. Those concerned will doubtless recognise themselves in what follows, (indeed some have sought publicity), but I stress my purpose is primarily to focus attention on the activities of the state, as a collection of competing agencies, for it is that aspect which is often overlooked, even by protagonists.

The most dramatic and public indication that Combat 18 is a phenomenon in which the state takes an interest was provided by John Tyndall, BNP leader, when on 14/12/93 he issued an *Organisers Bulletin* to trusted BNP members, intended to serve as "notice of complete repudiation of Combat 18 and declaring that group to be a hostile organisation" (p.1). Tyndall's case for the proscription of C18 rested on two counts — their antagonistic attitude towards the BNP leadership (including setting themselves up "as the disciplinary enforcement apparatus of the BNP" — p.1), and, most interestingly for current purposes, their alleged relationship to the state. He found it strange that C18 leaders have not been prosecuted either under the Public Order Act (for their advocacy of political force against opponents)[4] or on Race Relations charges.[5] Tyndall went on to say that even if it isn't known who exactly *produces* C18 publications it is difficult to imagine that there are not police infiltrators in C18, in which case "it would be truly amazing if those infiltrators were not able to inform the police of the precise identities of those responsible for breakages of the law and, more to the point, for the organising of those who break the law" (p.2). His explanation for this lack of action against C18 is that it is "astonishing, . . unless orders have come down from 'very high up' that Combat 18 is not to be touched because it is performing valuable services to the State — these valuable services being the sowing of discord and division within the ranks of nationalists" (p.2-3). By the time of January's *British Nationalist,* BNP leadership attitudes had hardened somewhat, with the declaration that "there is growing evidence to suggest that C18 has been heavily infiltrated, and probably taken over, by Government agents who are acting as '*agents provocateurs*' in order to incite nationalists into criminal activities, thereby making them vulnerable to arrest and imprisonment" (p.7). BNP leadership views are one thing, the attitudes of ordinary members another: personnel widely viewed as C18 have been recently witnessed on a variety of very public BNP events (such as electoral canvassing in the Isle of Dogs), with no apparent animosity.

Combat 18 — a brief history

A lot of questions are raised by Tyndall's analysis, and before dealing with them, a little elementary history about C18 is in order. The origins of C18 are a subject about which state-connected sources have peddled much disinformation.[6]

My investigations have found that C18 grew out of very real events and tendencies on the Right, much of their initial muscle/brains coming from disaffected ex-BM members who had dropped out when the BM wound down much public activity (although not the organisation) for a few years starting in 1984. Further spurs were two events occurring in 1991 — the fracas at the League of Saint George Kensington meeting, where clearly inadequate stewarding (from a fascist point of view) led to the gathering being well and truly turned over,[7] this being followed by the arrest and deportation of American 'Holocaust Denial' expert Fred Leuchter. Leuchter had been planning to speak at a meeting organised by David Irving and stewarded by Chris Marchant/Nick Griffin of the International Third Position, and the inability of those guarding the meeting to prevent his removal was remarked upon adversely. Both these occurrences were highly embarrassing, and led to C18 setting itself the task of providing fascists with two services: security/engaging in confrontation with "reds" on the one hand; and on the other "building up an intelligence network to monitor the reds and other enemies".[8] The latter activity was for a while performed through the medium of the publication *Redwatch*, the former by 'street actions' and the provision of 'troops' for a wide range of events. Another factor in the formation and self-confidence of C18 was the activities of Nazis abroad, especially in Germany. Events there seemed to show that not only could Nazis exert strong influence on mainstream agendas through violence against asylum-seekers, such actions didn't necessarily harm fascist electoral prospects, which were looking up. The idea that violence harmed electoral chances had been one of the guiding beliefs of the more reflective Far Right, and today still strongly affects the National Front and Third Way, as well as (very recently and hurriedly) the BNP leadership — hence their distancing from C18 described herein.[9]

Harold Covington — master of illusion?

Into this maelstrom of discontent, disaffection and readiness for 'action' stepped the rotund figure of Harold A Covington, 'National Socialist'. Some aspects of his involvement are still under investigation, about others we can be certain. For a start, the original *Redwatch* used Harold Covington's North Carolina address as a mail-drop, fully consistent with the task he had announced for himself when setting up his 'Resistance' network — a 'facilitator' for Nazis worldwide.[10] The reason for a US mail-drop would be to get round the Race Relations Acts, and (in theory at least) provide greater security.

Covington was given star billing in the *MI5 In Action* show as a guiding figure behind C18, something which led to his widely distributed *Open Letter To The British Left* (May 1993). In it, aside from (rather unconvincing) attempts to downplay the significance of stories about him personally, Covington tried to project the creation of C18 onto — the MI5-linked *Searchlight* magazine, right down to the production of fake stickers![11] Now, I don't doubt the capacity of the *Searchlight* team to engage in the most outrageous forgeries, but even they did not *invent* C18, and Covington knows it, thus his statement that there "is no such thing as C18" (p.1) can be dismissed.[12] Not content to leave matters there, Covington wrote another document in November 1993, less widely-circulated than the earlier one, entitled *The Great Combat 18 Hoax*. This was largely a tired repetition of the earlier one (with less humour), but there were serious points in it worthy of comment. Most noteworthy was the contention that an *intended* effect of the April *MI5 In Action* programme may have been the encouragement of some viewers to "take up the Combat 18 scenario in earnest and start actually fighting back against multi-racialism using that designation" (p.4). This may seem a wild conjecture, but isn't that surprising in the light of traditional spook procedure.[13] Covington also laid stress on *Searchlight's* MI5 links, but in a propagandistic and shallow way, adding little to previous knowledge. I am not sure just who Covington expected to be taken in by this production, clearly not readers of *The Order*. For issue 5 contained a news item stating "Combat 18 are now producing a deluxe version of *Redwatch*. Send 4 x 50p stamps to Dixie Press for sample copy".[14] The address given for Dixie Press turned out (again) to be one of Covington's — PO Box 608 Raleigh NC 27601 USA.[15] Sure enough, this is the address printed on the back of the glossy *C18* magazine, (on which more below).

Notes towards a revisionist interpretation of Covington

All the above indicates Covington to be occasionally anxious to deny his role in providing mail-drop facilities to C18, but doesn't necessarily show he has played a larger part than postal redirection. That however, would be rather less ambitious than the task he set himself when founding the 'Resistance Network'. Two things that might militate against a greater role for him are his supposed IRA sympathies, and the imputation widespread on the Right that he is an FBI asset. What, however, if Covington *were* a state asset: how might that fit in to the overall picture? While scant, the importance of the supposition means such evidence as there is on this score deserves rigorous examination.

The standard reference work on the US Right, by John George and Laird Wilcox, provides some clues. They outline how in 1979 Covington went to the HQ of the National Socialist Party of America (NSPA), and in the absence of leader Frank Collins discovered (in Covington's words) "films, pictures and addresses of some little boys", as a result of which "we handed Frank Collin to the cops on a silver platter".[16]

Personally, I would have thought there may have been far more appropriate ways of dealing with Collin than handing him over to the police, but there you have it. There is no dispute of Collins' guilt, though this doesn't end the matter. The photos and so on may have been in Collins office precisely because a state asset placed them there, having removed them from elsewhere? Whatever the mechanics, in 1980 Covington assumed the NSPA leadership himself. George and Wilcox comment that "his streak of successes was short-lived, however. Events during the trials of Klansmen and NSPA members led some of his followers to suspect he was an undercover informant. Faced with internal revolt and what he later called 'harassment & threats by the ATF,[17] Covington announced he was going underground. In March 1981 he appointed St. Louis NSPA leader Michael Allen, twenty nine, as his successor and disappeared shortly thereafter". George and Wilcox tell us that Allen turned out to be a "*bona fide* ATF informant" (p.362).

All this raises questions about Covington: at the very least, his judgement of character. But, that would hardly be surprising: for example nobody fingers John Tyndall as a state asset because he allowed Ray Hill (highly likely to have been a state asset himself: most probably Special Branch and later MI5) to occupy a position of prominence in the BNP.[18] The plot thickens however when we realise that Covington introduced not one but quite possibly *three* ATF informants into the neo-nazi movement. According to *Spotlight* 17/10/83, three "ATF undercover agents, Marshal Reece, Bernard Butkovich and Mike Sweat have now been officially identified". Joe Grady, a Klan leader, said that Covington's disappearance after the 1979 murder of five Leftist demonstrators at Greensboro North Carolina was because he was an "Anti-Defamation League pimp". Covington denied these charges, but from the outside, after all these years, it seems strange to me that Covington was never even charged with Greensboro, being identified during the trial as "an unindicted conspirator".[19] Was it the state protecting its own?

Covington's response to the above charges is, as far as I'm aware, to make light of them. In the *March Up Country* (1987) he simply refers to the alleged Jewish origin of the *Spotlight* writer, as though that disposed of the matter.[20] More seriously, he later in the same book refers to one of the three, Bernard Butkovitch, and says the following: "we had, in fact , already spotted Butkovitch as a plant and the last time he showed up at a Party meeting we were only constrained by the presence of reporters and TV cameras from confronting him with the evidence we had gathered" (p.73). Again, is this not strange — surely the presence of TV cameras would make it an *ideal* time to confront a state asset and make them squirm?

The above is suggestive, rather than conclusive, and I fully admit I haven't examined the whole affair in detail as yet, but I thought it useful to summarise the results of my enquiries thus far. As a result of these question marks against Covington, I re-read the coverage in the indisputably MI5-linked *Searchlight* magazine as a benchmark. There, I found something very curious: in the two major features on Covington, June 1992 and April 1993, little stress is laid on Covington possibly being a state asset. The June 1992 issue mentions an assertion by the (widely-discredited) late Ben Klassen (Church of the Creator) that "Covington might be a CIA operative" (p.5), but offers no opinion (unusual for *Searchlight* that). The April 1993 issue drops even mention of the CIA allegation. The whole effect of the two articles (and the *MI5 In Action* documentary of April 1993) was to *build up* Covington, not raise questions about his possible state connections. The June 1992 issue presents him as an 'enemy of the state', calling upon MI5 to throw him out of Britain; rare indeed for *Searchlight* to make demands upon their superiors like this. Given the first issue of *Redwatch* had come out three months earlier, in March, then assuming Covington was involved in advising the compilers, his work was already done. The great attention giving to exposing his residence at Palamos Road Leytonstone, complete with photograph, might just have been a big publicity stunt, designed to enhance his reputation with UK neo-nazis just before a pre-arranged departure. This is only conjecture, but why have not *Searchlight*, who boast of their extensive international 'network', ever brought before their readers the above questions I have raised? Is it their legendary sloppiness and disregard for the facts, or is there some other state-directed reason?

Assuming, for the sake of argument, that Covington might be an ATF/FBI asset, what would be the point? On one level, the answer is simple: the identity of those fascists writing to the USA, and the information sent, would all ultimately find its way back to the secret state over here. In which case, MI5 would have an access to top level information, *and* access to targetting opponents (via the FBI), that secret police persons normally only dream of. Covington himself can hardly complain that state control of mailing addresses is an unimportant issue: on 8/6/94 he issued a circular denouncing Tom and John Metzger of WAR (White Aryan Resistance) for colluding in just such a scam concerning their Fallbrook California PO Box. According to Covington (and he reproduces a letter which on the face of it substantiates his claims in full), "in order to continue living off their mail-order income from White racial nationalists who sent them money in good faith, Tom and John Metzger allowed Morris Dees[21] to use their box as a 'listening post' and intelligence-gathering point" (p.1). So, this might explain the mechanism, and maybe MI5's motives are evident throughout this text: but what of the FBI? A clue there can be found in the *Intelligence Newsletter* for 13/1/94 (p.7). They refer to the fact that on a trip to Europe in December 1993, FBI Director Louis Freeh didn't just talk about the mafia. On 15/12/93 he met Hans Ludwig Zachert and other high BKA (German Intelligence) officials, and discussed the issue of FBI-BKA co-operation against neo-nazis on both sides of the Atlantic. In other words, like MI5, the FBI is seeking to expand its remit into other areas, as well as 'monitoring' existing ones. In that respect, it would be highly cost-effective budgetary wise to have engaged in a little prior investment to solidify the links one later 'investigates'. Which is where Covington (just like Hepple before him) just *might* come in. I do not know for sure: I suggest you make up your own mind, on the balance of probability. At the present time, he seems to have abandoned the idea of cell structures, and is in the process of building yet another nazi group, the 'National Socialist Workers People's Party'. His memory seems to have undergone yet another reorientation since he denied C18 existed (in November 1993): the August 1994 edition of *Resistance* refers in a matter of fact way to having corresponded with two prison "members of the Combat 18 group . . . a completely clandestine organisation" (p.7). Fancy that!

What does seem unquestionable is that the US neo-nazi movement is full of spook assets. For example, Dennis Mahon, who wrote an amusing article in WAR newspaper on 'How To Expose An Agent' (May 1994), turns out, according to an interview given to a writer for the La Rouche publication *Executive Intelligence Review* on 18/1/93, to have been a sometime operative of US naval intelligence, an anti-Castro special operations agent, and a *collaborator* with the East German secret police, the STASI, from at least 1988.[22]   David Duke, another prominent (reformed?) neo-nazi, was according to the 1990 biography by Michael Zatarain a CIA operative in Laos. If you add to this the question marks against the Metzgers, not as assets, but in terms of allowing access to their mail box by the 'enemy', then the US is a political minefield. As Covington never tires of pointing out, the US Nazi scene seems to be full of kooks, spooks, sexual perverts and Hollywood nazis. Is he one of them? I await further evidence both for and against, and would welcome it from any quarter. In the meantime, I would have thought that all parties involved can draw their own provisional conclusions.

Notes:

1   *Spearhead* 305 July 1994 p.6.

2   Issue 20 May 1993 p.10. The change in editorship of *League Sentinel* later in the year may well have brought yet another policy switch against such co-operation. A potential indication of this was the suggestion in a more recent *League Sentinel* (issue 23 March 1994) that individuals on the Far Right should strongly consider suing the police on occasions of wrongful detention (p.11/13). This has been done, with some success to date.

3   September 1994 p.2.

4   p.2 the relevant section being Chapter 6 Section 2 (1b).

5   p.2 again, relevant legislation being Public Order Act 1986 part III Section 19. *C18* statements that might come into this category are the calls for execution of Jews and "white race mixers". Tyndall's mention of this legislation could be (and was) seen by some as encouraging the police to prosecute individuals.

6   See *The Genesis of Combat 18*, a document submitted by *Searchlight* to the Home Affairs Select Committee 'Sub-Committee to Inquire into Racial Attacks and Harassment' 1993 for the prime example. *Searchlight* admit their state connections more and more as time goes by, whether it be in editor Gable's oral evidence to the Committee in December, when he called for MI5 to 'investigate' C18, and asserted (ludicrously) that those subjected

to fire-bombing/murder "would be better protected if MI5 took over", supplementing this with exactly the line I had predicted he would take, "that a shift to MI5 would make sense because . . . Combat 18 had links with Northern Irish terrorists like the UDA" (both quotes from the London *Evening Standard* 9/12/93), see also *Independent* 9/12/93, as well as the January editorial of *Searchlight*, where the call was repeated, this time to include either "the Police National Intelligence Bureau, or . . . MI5 and MI6" (p.2). This presumably is the same MI6 which *Searchlight* have been telling us over the years is working hand in glove with fascist fugitive 'terrorists' like Roberto Fiore . . . How exactly this is meant to be squared with the specious denunciations of *agents provocateurs* on page 20 of the same issue (specious given Hepple's as yet unexplained antics) — well, we aren't told. For after all, are not agencies like MI5 and MI6 *precisely* those who run *agents provocateurs* in the first place? In which case, calling upon them to 'investigate' paramilitary formations amongst fascists would be laughable if it wasn't so serious. The sad thing is, although *Searchlight* are well aware that among some sectors of the Left their 'number is up', others delude themselves that *Searchlight's* relationship to the state is merely one of 'passing information' (the apparent view of the revived *Black Flag* — rather less prescient than their predecessor . . .).

Those who affect to find my views on *Searchlight* 'exaggerated' or 'far-fetched' need to adequately account for the fact that so far (September), *ten* months after *At War With The Truth* (AWWT) was published, they have not even dared to *refer* to it, never mind refute it. Instead, they have chosen to concoct ever more bizarre (and malign) fantasies connecting me personally to Ulster Loyalists, C18 and drug-dealing. Furthermore, critics also need to explain just how it was, if I have got *Searchlight* wrong, that their verbal evidence to the Select Committee in December (on which date their written evidence was released too), should so accurately conform to the outlines I had predicted in Appendix 3 of AWWT written at the end of *October*. The call for MI5/MI6 to take over 'investigation' of C18 is one that *Searchlight* said "might astonish some of our readers" (January Editorial) but it will have come as no surprise to readers of my work. *Searchlight* (and other state-connected sources) cannot be ignored because they are so important — both in this country and abroad. There is virtually no competing analysis of C18 other than mine; virtually all the potted accounts trotted out by Leftist groups (and often the media) are derived from *Searchlight* (and thus MI5) or Special Branch, whether attributed or not. The evidence given to the Select Committee by the Anti-Racist Alliance and the Board of Deputies of British Jews said little of substance about C18, and *CARF* now provides virtually no hard analysis about current fascist strategy, for reasons best known to themselves. *That* is why *Searchlight* is so useful to state agencies, and the vital importance of an accurate, non-state-compromised understanding of contemporary fascism, is precisely why *Searchlight* needs to be put out of business once and for all, with a stake firmly driven into its political heart (figuratively speaking).

7 *The Order* issue 1 April 1993 p.9, one of two interviews given by C18 to the Far Right press to date.

8 *Thor-Would* 4 December 1992 p.10.

9 It is widely believed by Nazis that the BNP were involved in the sabotage of the Ian Stuart Donaldson Memorial Concert in January 1994 — see *Putsch* 9 February 1994 on this.

Another factor behind the increase in support for groups like C18 and hard-line Nazi publications like the *Oak, Thor-Would, The Order, Putsch,* and indeed the revitalised British Movement, is an impatience with what are seen as esoteric and failed 'ideological deviations' from/'dilutions' of Nazism, as chronicled in my on-going series of articles for *Lobster* starting with issue 23.

10   The introductory bulletin *What Is The Resistance Network* outlined three main functions: "to provide a contact point and bulletin board for the world-wide movement . . . to provide quality standardised samizdat literature", and finally "to provide a think-tank and consultancy for the individual activity units which will organise and encourage Movement-wide debate on strategy, tactics and ideology".

11   p.2.

12   Appendix 1 of *At War With The Truth* reprints a C18 document (*Collecting Information On The Enemy*) using Covington's address, Appendix 3 an example of what I take to be a particularly sickening anti-semitic forgery.

13   The assertion that Gerry Gable used his influence to get Special Branch to raid Alexander Baron and seize his files, because he had mentioned Sonia Hochfelder, is unlikely: such a raid is likely to have been carried out on behalf of others.

14   p.8.

15   See for example *Resistance* November 1993 p.8.

16   Quoted p.361 of Lloyd George/Laird Wilcox *Communists Nazis Klansmen & Others on the Fringe* Prometheus Buffalo New York 1992 p.361 Collins served 3 years of a 7 year jail sentence.

17   Bureau of Alcohol Tobacco and Firearms, part of the FBI. The agency under whose auspices murder was carried out at Waco Texas in early 1993.

18   Perhaps Mr Hill and his controllers might care to sue me on this point, as he has threatened. That way, the full glory of his career and the fictional Notting Hill bomb plot can be discussed in open court.

19   *Spotlight* 30/4/84.

20   p.27 published by Liberty Bell publications Reedy West Virginia.

21   An anti-Nazi Southern lawyer.

22   *Executive Intelligence Review* 5/11/93 p.37 in September 1993 it was reported that Mahon was planning to visit the UK, but he didn't. See the *Independent on Sunday* 5/9/93.

Combat 18 and the state

WITH THE BASIC BACKGROUND in mind, I will now turn to the complicated bit — where MI5, and Special Branch too (in my estimation) become active players. The first public indication that the state was taking a close interest in C18 were the arrests of 376 fascists (and Loyalists) who gathered in January 1993 to protest against the annual 'Bloody Sunday' commemoration march in Central London. Those arrested were detained by the police, questioned, and in some cases had their photographs taken — with virtually no charges being proferred. Most Leftist commentators downplayed this event, missing its significance as an exercise primarily in *intelligence-gathering*, the legal basis for the operation being unclear and questionable.[1] Basic information about the personnel likely to be involved in C18-type activity having been gathered, and putative 'assets' pencilled in, it was now time for action. What I mean by 'action' here is the secret state feeding in information about targets for the Far Right to focus on and attack, as well as (on occasion) using personnel to carry out attacks themselves; in the process sowing discord among all factions on the political scene, Right and Left. I do not intend here to spend much time on the episodes/details outlined in two earlier productions,[2] except inasmuch as they relate to the overall picture, and hope to look at new elements, things not dwelt on before.

The primary way in which the state has sought to influence fascist hit-squads is, as I've suggested, steering them in the direction of targets to attack, without fascists necessarily knowing they have been so manipulated.[3] Take for example the two attacks and a robbery which have taken place on the anarchist bookshop 'Freedom' in Whitechapel East London, starting 27/3/93. In an interview with C18 published in *The Order* April 1993, that went to press *before* the attack, C18 referred to attacks personnel had suffered outside their homes. They stated "we have evidence to suggest that these attacks are being carried out by a London anarchist group based in Whitechapel"[4] Inquiries have elicited the information that C18 believed this group to be Class War. I have no idea whether CW were involved in such (alleged) attacks; more to the point is that CW have *no* association with Freedom Books (in fact the only connection is that they briefly used the address for mailing purposes nearly ten years ago till they were thrown out). This raises the question: who provided such bogus information to C18 in the first place? After the first and well-publicised attack on Freedom, C18 took the unusual step of denying they had been involved[5] — which may have been because they were not involved or realised, *after* the event, that they had been gulled into doing somebody else's dirty work. For the date of the attack, 27/3, was exactly a day before the spate of media stories linking Red Action to the INLA/IRA began, thus making this action seem to fit somebody's script in terms of escalating political conflict. The issue of *New Statesman & Society* immediately after the attack on Freedom speculated that "the main suspicion is that the real quarry was not Freedom but Class War . . . which has been involved in direct battles with fascists, but which has no premises to attack". This speculation was remarkably prescient, but was supplemented by the outrageous claim that "the gang may even have belonged to one of the factions into which Class War recently split".[6] Now, that *is* a startling piece of speculation that some might see as disinformation, which even on the basis of the article it appeared in is highly illogical: why should Class War (any faction) attack a premises nothing to do with them, whatever perceived differences with Freedom? The purpose of such a 'planted' item was clearly to hype up conflict within anarchist circles, and the month of April saw the spurious naming of anarchist Tim Scargill as a Nazi by *Searchlight*.[7] Parallel to this infighting *within* the Left, and the possible relationship to the targetting of Red Action, the Freedom Bookshop attacks were also aimed at setting fascists and anarchists at one another's throats. The rationale for this was summed up by one bookshop (that has itself been under attack) as the state maintaining "control by using the 'extremists' to neutralise one another, gaining the upper hand to get seriously busy dismantling the 'alternative' scene".[8] This escalation of political conflict, and encouragement of total confusion as to its origins and dynamics, is a tried and trusted weapon in the arsenal of the secret state — *intoxication*.[9] MI5/*Searchlight* agent Hepple was particularly active around this time, spreading lies to *Green Anarchist* circles that both the *Morning Star* offices and the SWP's London Bookshop Bookmarks had been burnt down.[10]

When it comes to placing individuals on the 'agenda', *Target* seems to have been a publication the state has sought to influence. I have before commented on the fact that Tim Scargill of Class War featured in *Target* issue 2, at the same time as he was denounced by *Searchlight* as an anarcho-nazi *agent provocateur* (without foundation).[11] Exactly the same cycle of events seems to have occurred with another anarchist anti-fascist (skinhead), 'Tony H', who has spent time in Sweden as well as other Scandinavian countries, getting involved in radical politics there.[12] He featured in issue 3 and 4 of *Target* as well as the *C18* magazine, and was attacked by a large group of fascists in August 1993, having a paving-stone slab thrown at his head. Now, given he is an anti-fascist skinhead, that in itself might well be reason enough for fascists to 'have a go' at him, but in an uncanny echo of events concerning Scargill a year earlier, he found his full name mentioned in *Searchlight* January 1994 (p.20) where he was described (to my knowledge without foundation) as an "alleged anti-fascist" undertaking a "strategy of involving innocent young anti-fascists in criminal acts"[13]

Exactly why Tony Haughian should have been targetted by a state-connected organ such as *Searchlight* is a moot question — my view (having now met him) is that in his travels in Scandinavia or Yorkshire (see below) he (inadvertently) came across some kind of state operation, and it was felt necessary to discredit him before he disclosed such. The extensive coverage given to Sweden on the same page hints at this, and the activities of the Swedish VAM (*Vitt Ariski Motstand*),strike me at first sight as classic examples of what the secret state would set up a 'pseudo-gang' to do.[14] The country that may provide the key to the victimisation of Tony Haughian, at least from the state's perspective, is Denmark. The same article in January's *Searchlight* that attacked him also made a series of outrageous and utterly false allegations about activists in Copenhagen Anti-Fascist Action. Harmless fireworks they had brought along were described by *Searchlight* as *plastic explosives*, and legitimate activists described as *agents provocateurs*. Not only is this grossly untrue, and refuted by Copenhagen AFA in their letter to *Searchlight* of 10/2/94, circulated by them on 24/5, having received no right of reply or apology,[15] there are sinister forces at work here. First, it ill behoves *Searchlight* and their MI5 superiors to accuse *anybody* of *agent provocateur* activity, especially given they have never explained the antics of Hepple satisfactorily, nor even Ray Hill or Dave Roberts come to that, of the so-far disclosed assets. Secondly, this attack by *Searchlight* seems to be fully consistent with a Europe-wide attempt to criminalise the militant wing of the anti-fascist movement and autonomous radicals generally. Radical anti-Maastricht campaigners in Denmark have been the subject of marked police brutality, especially in the Norrebro district of Copenhagen on the night following the (unfortunately successful) referendum of 18/5/93.[16] What better way to deflect attention from Danish police brutality than to peddle lies about anti-fascists? And what better publication to peddle those lies in than the 'International Pro-State Monthly' *Searchlight*?

Turning again to the targetting of groups, it is noteworthy that the information in *Target* issue 2 on Class War, while it was no doubt accurate at the time of compilation, was about 50% out of date by the time of publication. This pattern of accurate but dated information, bespeaks to me of having been lying around in state files for a couple of years. Again, as with the earlier attempts to entrap *Green Anarchist* into publishing bogus lists of fascists, the whole point of such operations is that those who print the information, and carry out attacks don't know on whose behalf they are doing so, or even that there *are* ulterior agendas at work. Indeed, for them to be aware that their actions coincide with state agendas would be highly counter-productive for the state, as the number of *conscious* state agents in both the Far Right and Far Left is miniscule proportionately, and if attention was to be focussed directly on the state then the implications for MI5 and Special Branch, as well as their assets, would be none too healthy.[17] Another very suspicious matter, this time concerning monitoring of post, is worthy of note. In their main body of written evidence to the Select Committee, which textual scrutiny indicates was submitted April/May 1993, *Searchlight* disclosed the address of *Target* was 'Andrew Jones PO Box 2054 South Vineland New Jersey 08360 USA' (in fact the name/address of a Ku Klux Klan faction).[18] This fact wasn't disclosed publicly in the UK till late in the year, the gap being accounted for, in my view, by the desire to allow the FBI (and thus MI5) to continue to monitor the post going there, a highly understandable reticence on the part of a state annexe, not otherwise. The above may seem a minor point, but it is by close attention to such nuances that the outlines of state inputs into politics can be discerned.[19]

Combat 18 — the next generation?

Now let us turn to the latest publication ostensibly to come from C18, the glossy *C18* magazine circulating December 1993: which was the trigger for Tyndall's wrath. It is a peculiar publication, and while I don't doubt that it was produced with the *permission* of 'Mark I' C18, it marks a qualitative shift in language and content from earlier offerings. Although it is not as *consistently* 'extreme' as the White Wolves document, it has been much more widely disseminated, and is of greater importance therefore. While not alone in its advocacy of 'cell structures', it is so inflammatory as to almost invite prosecution, with its injunction to readers to acquire "a basic knowledge of military small arms. This is essential! Improvised explosives + basic infantry methods. Find out about them — now!" The idea that "cells must remain self sufficient. They will be guided by C18 and when the time to come out is here thay shall be told" begs the question as to who is to decide *when* this is, and how orders are to be transmitted for such, and indeed how cells are supposed to *differentiate* between genuine calls to arms and bogus ones. The publication couldn't be more wrong when it argues that the "cell structure is the security forces biggest nightmare. They cannot infiltrate! They cannot destroy a whole movement!". All the state has to do is either use *long term* agents to infiltrate cells, or (even simpler) set them up itself. It is after all, a mixture of both methods that was used by Patrick Daly to set up Heffernan and McMonagle. While the document draws attention to an FBI *agent provocateur* (Joe Allen) in the Church of the Creator in the USA,[20] it doesn't mention Allen's equivalent here, Tim Hepple. Hepple, need I remind some of you, was *very* keen on 'cell structures'.[21] Furthermore, another person (BNP member Peter Rushden) widely seen as a state agent, who was rather poorly defended by John Tyndall in the *Organisers Bulletin* already cited, and in whom I take a personal interest[22] isn't mentioned here either, when had this been a 'Mark I' C18 production he surely would have been. For a magazine that purports to emanate from C18 pure and simple, this publication is rather short on Nazi symbolism, surprisingly, not one swastika to be seen — but plenty of AWB imagery. All the above things lead me to suspect that this magazine wasn't a production of 'Mark I' C18, even though they may have (as well as others) played a part in its distribution.

Assuming, for the sake of argument, that this magazine was largely *written* by 'Mark II' C18 personnel, stepping into the organisational vacuum mentioned earlier, what might the significance of this be? At the very least, it can be conjectured that this magazine causes severe problems for 'Mark I' C18, inasmuch as they will be widely held to be responsible, and a possible defence that they produced earlier *Redwatches* but not this 'deluxe version' *C18* would be to admit earlier (quite probably) illegal publications, not very wise at all.[23] If the 'Mark II' writers of this magazine don't believe in Nazism, it raises the question as to just what they *do* believe in, if anything. The 'Aims of C18' section, referring to their desire to "ship all non-whites back to Africa, Asia, Arabia, alive or in body bags, the choice is theirs", and putting Jews not immediately executed "into camps until we find a final solution for the eternal Jew", does not strike me as the stuff of fascists who actually think they can *win*, or of those who are clever at avoiding breaches of the law. The idea of building an 'alternative business infrastructure' does seem plausible (and familiar): sections of this document could certainly have been written by an intelligent and articulate (but foul-mouthed) fascist. There is though, more to it than that in my opinion. Parts of this publication (a collective endeavour), frankly, read like they were penned by state agents with the express purpose of discrediting C18. There could be another, even more sinister motive, that of 'setting people up'. The idea would be to either plant arms/ammunition/explosives (as in the USA) or even offer them to enthusiastic readers (recruits), and then pounce on those ensnared for possession/use of such, using the contents of publications like this as a 'justification'. This wouldn't be the first time: and in the light of the entrapment/escalation operations carried out by MI5 outlined in earlier chapters, is a distinct possibility. This may (or may not) be related to recent reports of the use of commercial explosives by Ulster Loyalists. We shall see.

In the meantime, various victim groups/individuals who may be a 'problem' to the state will have been 'dealt with' According to the *Jewish Chronicle*, the publication has already been referred to the Crown Prosecution Service and the police, and in the *Observer* (6/3/94) David Rose (who else!) wrote about the publication under the salient headline 'Neo-nazis briefed on forming armed cells'. The ubiquitous Ken Hyder too got in on the act, referring (without proof of course) to C18 as the "former armed wing" of the BNP.[24] In *At War With The Truth*, I suggested[25] that the dummy Nazi fanzine *Einherjar* was most probably an attempt to influence the workings of the Home Affairs Select Committee, (even though not openly submitted), by seeming to connect Loyalists and Fascists operationally.[26] The appearance of the *C18* magazine, at the start of December just before non-governmental organisations gave verbal evidence, may or may not have been coincidence: but the timing can certainly have done no harm at all to those postulating the imminent likelihood of armed violence from fascists. A distinct possibility is that what may be going on now, and even more in the near future, is supplanting of the C18 'Mark I' leadership by others, perhaps to be facilitated by the medium of arrests (for political and non-political offences), including framings — watch this space! In different ways, this process seems to have happened both to the original Red Brigades in Italy[27] and the Irish People's Liberation Organisation in Northern Ireland, therefore we cannot say it couldn't happen here. Indeed, in the light of events elsewhere in the political spectrum, attempted entrapment and personnel replacement seem to be very much on the agenda. Some on the fascist fringe are, however, developing an increasing awareness of the ubiquitous and sinister influence of MI5 on their 'patch', as evidenced perhaps in the document *Satanlight no. 666: C11/13 & the Ginger Fish: the Terror Squad Reds*, rumoured to be the handiwork of Steve Sargent. The pertinent question though, is will activists on the neo-nazi Right wake up fully before they end up in jail: or dead?

Tyndall's argument revisited

Concerning Tyndall's suggestion, that C18 are some sort of state-licensed front, we are now in a position to better put it into perspective. Firstly, he is being highly disingenuous, when in the past he was quite happy to accept C18 protection at meetings and rallies, and has been frequently photographed in the company of people associated with C18. It is patently undeniable that some of those involving themselves in C18/C18-style activities have included/do include well-known members of his own party, including organisers. Although some of these people may well have joined the BNP while their primary political loyalties lay elsewhere, that's a different matter, made all the more likely by the lack of real political debate inside an organisation that doesn't even have Annual General Meetings, only 'Rallies'. Secondly, for him to categorise the *C18* magazine as state-oriented just because it is glossy is a poor argument, it doesn't cost *that* much to produce glossy publications, especially in bulk.[28] Thirdly, the timing of Tyndall's bulletin, shortly after the (September) Beackon by-election victory in the Isle of Dogs, and even sooner after the release from prison of Tony Lecomber, who sided with the BNP leadership (rather than C18 as some expected), points to a rebuttal based more on conjuncture than principle.[29] Following Beackon's success, Tyndall believes the 'call from the Palace' might be around the corner, in preparation for which hypothetical eventuality he has come to the realisation that (unlike the very recent past) the "BNP must cease to be a 'street gang' and become a serious political party" (p.3), in pursuance of which the BNP is to downgrade demonstrations, a radical shift from the policy adhered to as late as January 1993. In *British Nationalist* for that month, a front page article proclaimed "a party like the BNP must first win power on the streets if it is to achieve power at the ballot box" — very clear, that. In this situation, the BNP leadership has staked all on elections, and doesn't (for the moment) *need* significant numbers of the street-fighters they were until recently happy to be associated with.[30] The BNP's showing in the May council elections did not perturb them unduly, even the loss of Beackon's seat, given his increased vote, and so the 'electoral road' is still on the immediate horizon.[31] While Tyndall was disappointed with only 7% of the vote in the Dagenham by-election in June, this did make him the first ever BNP parliamentary candidate to retain a deposit, and the BNP took further heart from their showing at Shadwell (East

London) where they were narrowly beaten into third place by the Liberals in ward they hadn't fought before.

C18, the BNP & the media: some observations

I can well believe C18 did, as stated, ask "to meet Tyndall on six separate occasions" only for him to pull "out at the last moment" on each occasion,[32] and it has been widely reported that there was a 'clear the air' meeting around the time of the Dagenham by-election. This must put in perspective the various press reports speaking of a state of 'civil war' between the BNP and C18, as propagated particularly by Ken Hyder (*Evening Standard* 11/5/94) and Dennis Rice/Mark Porter *Sunday Express* 1/5/94) and finally Vivek Chaudhary and Owen Bowcott (*Guardian* 5/5/94). All three are clearly sourced by *Searchlight*, Rice & Porter preferring for some strange reason not to acknowledge this, attributing their opinions to an un-named 'Nazi watcher'. Is this perhaps because the *Express* has a libel case pending in which *Searchlight* are involved? How sad! The content of all three articles covers much the same ground. Attacks on BNP Press Officer Michael Newland in late April 1994, and BNP Newham election candidate Michael Davidson and an incendiary device at the BNP's Welling HQ are all (incorrectly in my view) described as having been carried out by 'C18'. Other attacks on the BNP, such as that on Tony Lecomber in January 1994 and Eddie Butler in late 1993 and April 1994, were described by Tyndall as having been carried out by "an individual associated with C18. But he's working on his own"[33]

What particularly interests me for current purposes is one of the attacks *falsely* attributed to 'C18', that of 7/4/94 on their Welling HQ, in which party worker Alf Waite was injured.[34] The gross inaccuracy that it may have been C18 (or the BNP themselves) was repeated across the Left: for example *Militant* speculated the BNP might have carried out the attack on themselves to gain publicity (15/4/94). *CARF* were sadly little better, as late as July attributing Welling to C18.[35] Even the *Order* (Editorial issue 7) attributed the bombing to unspecified "Reds", the inference being they meant Red Action. In fact, all the above were wrong: the Welling bomb was claimed by the militant animal rights group the 'Justice Department' (JD) in a press release that was put out by the ALF Press Officer on 20/4/94. The text of the JD's claim (which Robin Webb received anonymously as he does all claims) said that the JD "recognise that oppression of all individuals is wrong, whether they be human or non-human. Each individual deserves the right to live their lives without let or hindrance or any form of prejudice against them. On most 'animal rights' demonstrations and marches one can hear the chant 'Human Freedom, animal rights, one struggle, one fight'. The Justice Department wishes to make clear that this is not just empty rhetoric"[36] While I can understand the far Right getting the attribution wrong, there is little excuse for the press *as a whole* doing so. What we're talking here is deliberate *disinformation* being spread by *Searchlight* but willingly colluded in by the journalists named above, from whom *CARF* and *Militant* etc. will have culled their stories. I actually wasted my time writing a short letter to the *Guardian* the day after their mistaken attribution of Welling, but it wasn't printed. Papers like the *Guardian* and to a lesser extent the *Independent*, play a crucial role in policing the parameters of 'acceptable' political dissent. Certain views, like my own, are just too sharp to be printed and thereby legitimised. Instead, the *Guardian* in particular, in the area of 'fascism' has been disgraceful in its long-standing and uncritical recycling of whatever *Searchlight* and their MI5 associates feed to them. The purpose of suppressing the truth about the Justice Department's claim of Welling would seem clear to me (and I make no value judgement here): to deprive them of any credibility they might have gained among some anti-fascists for having carried out such an attack. Further, to avoid discussion about any anti-fascist strategies other than the 'electoral' road or petition-signing and lollipop-waving.

The Organisers' Bulletin *reviewed*

Situating all these shenanigans in the context of state activity, the December 1993 *Organisers Bulletin* reads like Tyndall could have got inside information from some-where inside the state apparatus. The obvious candidates would be Special Branch, whom it is reported Tyndall meets with frequently. For if it is the case (as I believe) that it is MI5's agenda to push the fascists in a violent direction, then this wouldn't necessarily please SB. Not so much out of a principled objection (although there may be an element of that), but because it wasn't Special Branch doing it. It might be objected that SB would never contemplate the hyping up of violence, as this would create more work for themselves, but especially in the current climate, some work is better than none, for them as for MI5. Perhaps understandably, Tyndall didn't distinguish between those *originally* involved in C18 and those who may have become involved more recently, it might even be he isn't as such aware of the ongoing power-shift. From our point of view though, retaining sight of such a distinction is the key to events that may unfold. On currently available evidence, therefore, I must say I see no reason to doubt the political independence from the state of the 'Mark I' C18 leadership, and also those responsible at a top level for producing *Target*, the recently-renamed 'Searchlight Victims' Support Group'. Thus, Tyndall's general argument that C18 as such are a state-licensed front is incorrect, however politically tempting it might be to believe otherwise! But, Tyndall *is right* in another sense — it is not too fanciful to suggest that C18 (as with the BNP) contains increasing numbers of state agents, who are biding their time, and seeking to turn it in practise (as opposed to rhetoric) towards the 'terrorist' direction sketched out in the *C18* magazine, but devised elsewhere by other interests.

In recent times, the last few months, at least half a dozen fascists presumed to be in/near to C18 have been 'approached' by people they *believe* to be Special Branch (who may be SB *or* MI5), and offered cash inducements to 'turn'. These people are only those that have rejected the offers — those who accepted will not have advertised such, and assets forced to work for the state because of financial/sexual reasons wouldn't talk about it either.

Street-fighting men?

While public order matters are not directly the province of MI5, events on the streets clearly affect the overall climate in which their agents operate, and for the purposes of current strategy, an intense escalation of conflict, combined with draconian curtailing of legal street activity would seem to be the optimal situation, narrowing down the parameters of political choice for the committed. Public order problems might seem like a honeypot of job creation for Special Branch, less so for MI5. From the latter's point of view, a multiplicity of loosely organised underground groups provide great scope for intervention manipulation and hopefully control, up to and including executions of state opponents by proxies. Rising street tension however, can suit both SB (job creation) and MI5 (driving some activists to 'extreme' action as a result of police curtailment of above-ground operations). That borne in mind, the ease with which the BNP were, following Beackon's election, banned from selling papers at Brick Lane in East London, where they had sold papers for years, even up to and including mass preventive arrests of fascists to prevent them travelling there, is disturbing, however much it may have been welcomed by the Anti-Nazi League.[37]. The recent stopping and searching of fascists in the Brick Lane area by police, including them being video-filmed, certainly wasn't carried out for any benign reason. I cannot over-emphasise the point that measures used against the fascists are later used against the Left, and, in terms of what traps may be in store for those in C18's orbit, mechanisms (such as entrapment) that have been used against the Left (and Greens as will be mentioned below) are equally liable to be used against the Far Right. The events surrounding the attempted 'Blood and Honour' gig for the late Ian Stewart Donaldson[38] in London on 15/1/94 do seem to show the police are adopting a hard line against both anti-fascists and fascists alike on the streets — for reasons best known to themselves, which surely cannot be due to cost reasons alone.[39]

MI5 and fascists — summing up

Moving back to the national picture again, the conclusion which should be drawn from the above excursion into the murky world of the Far Right is that it is an area in which the secret state has a very definite interest — and many fascists, by their propensity to engage in violence as a political strategy, leave themselves wide open to manipulation by the very forces of the state many of them (in their own minds) oppose.[40] Tying all the different strands together, there can be little better conclusion than that reached by the Italian anarchist Sanguinetti in 1979, speaking of Italy after the Aldo Moro kidnap. He was a keen observer of the transformation of the Red Brigades into a 'Mark II' front for the Italian secret state, and was himself falsely and absurdly accused of involvement with the BR. This, I believe, is the 'ideal type' future gameplan MI5 has in mind for C18, and I shall quote it at length:

"in the case of a small terrorist group spontaneously formed, there is nothing in the world easier for the detached corps of the state than to infiltrate it, and, thanks to the means they dispose of, and the extreme freedom of maneouvre which they enjoy, to get near the original summit, and to substitute themselves there, either by specific arrests activated at the right moment, or threough the assassination of the original leaders, which, as a rule, occurs after an armed conflict with the 'forces of order', forewarned about such an operation by their infiltrated elements.

From then on, the parallel services of the State find they have, at their disposal, a perfectly efficient organism to do as they please with, composed of naive or fanatical militants, which asks for nothing other than to be directed. The original little terrorist group changes strategists and becomes nothing other than a *defensive* appendage of the state, which maneouvres it with the utmost agility and ease".[41]

While imprisonment is more likely than death, Sanguinetti's hypothesis has some validity, I feel, not for the bulk of the Far Right, but for those inclined towards organised violence. The script has been read out: let the drama begin. There is no saying the government is either aware of, or approves, such a scenario. Government ministers have consistently rejected greater legislation to make racial harassment a specific crime,[42] The Home Affairs Select Committee, whose report into racial attacks and harassment was issued 25/5/94, are very much in favour of legislation.[43] More relevantly for this book's current purposes, and ironically in my view, the Committee's Report stated "we are aware of the involvement of the Security Service and the National Criminal Intelligence Service . . . we urge the police, Special Branch and the Security Service to continue to monitor extreme right-wing groups, and to continue to share information about these groups" (p. xxvi). That MI5 and Special Branch may not just be 'monitoring' but actively *participating* in, and seeking to use such groups, this is a possibility these parliamentarians are incapable of comprehending.

Notes:

1 The London-based newsletter *Contraflow*, in issue 5 March 1993, was one of the few publications to see the danger in this. As they commented, "there is no reason to believe that they will only use the tactic of mass preventative arrests against fascists. Indeed this tactic is a natural progression from that recently seen on anti-fascist events, where police have effectively detained people by surrounding them and refusing to let anybody leave". This was a tactic extensively used during the miners' strike of 1984-5, and the NF suffered from it too around that time.

2   *A Lie Too Far* and *At War With The Truth* — both MINA publications (1993)],

3   Given that both *Target* and before it *Redwatch*, have welcomed information from a wide variety of sources, including anonymously, then it would beggar belief to imagine state agents *hadn't* sent them information!

4   p.10.

5   See *League Sentinel* 20 May 1993 p.3

6   Shoreditch column 2/4/93 p.6. I have been informed that the column on this occasion was written by Jolyon Jenkins: a journalist who has received the rare accolade of being praised in *Searchlight*. Small world . . .

7   I am not questioning the integrity of NSS, a publication that has over the years acquitted themselves very well in covering the secret state, and has even mentioned my research favourably (15/10/93).

8   *Fascists, Anarchos & The Secret State*, put out by 121 Bookshop June 1993.

9   See Pierre Nord *L'Intoxication: Arme Absolute de la Guerre Subversive* Paris 1970 especially p.vii-x/5-7.

10 I am not doubting the former suffered an arson attack: but that is not the same as being burnt down, is it?

11 *Searchlight* April 1993 p.14.

12 For instance, taking part in an anti-racist occupation of the Danish Parliament (*Folketing*) in 1991.

13 p.20. *Searchlight* did not (of course) mention he had been attacked *by* fascists. See the reply 'Statement by Tony H' put out by the Hackney Anti-Fascist Co-ordinating Committee January 1994. The role of *CARF* magazine in this affair reeks of political cowardice. When he was attacked by fascists in August 1993 they covered the story (September/October 1993). Good. When however, *Searchlight* actually named him, something fascists had never done (and his name, Haughian, is an unusual one), *CARF didn't think this worthy of mention.* Yet is the targetting of an anti-fascist made any more acceptable when it is carried out by state-connected forces rather than the fascists themselves? On this evidence, *CARF* would appear to think so: or at least they lack the political guts and honesty to say otherwise in print. To paraphrase their September 1993 issue, 'anti-fascists need to take note of this'.

14 See *At War With The Truth* p.11-12 on this concept. The activities of *VAM* are well covered in the careful article by Helene Loow 'The Cult of Violence', p.62-79 in T Bjorgo and Rob Witte (ed) *Racist Violence In Europe* (Macmillan 1993).

15 *Searchlight* said they didn't believe in right of reply for AFA because "they are sick in their heads and a bunch of lunatics" (24/5 letter p.1).

16 See *Statewatch* July/August 1994 p.17-18 & especially *Fortress Europe?* Blomstervagen) Sweden September 1994 p.3-7 for a full account.

17 One of the many factors that has led to an upsurge in UDA/UFF violence since Brian Nelson was outed as an MI5 agent has been the urge on the part of the new leadership to distance themselves from the recent past of the UDA. As regards targetting, getting people/groups *put on* agendas is a far easier thing to do than getting them *taken off,* in that case advance warning is given to (selected) individuals — and those not 'in favour' are not warned at all. For an example of the former phenomenon (prior notice), issue 4 of *Target*

named those involved in Central books, the main distributors of *Searchlight* (and *Lobster*). When the individuals were contacted shortly after it came out, to warn them, reports reaching me indicate they already knew, and weren't perturbed. Many of the details printed were significantly out of date, these two things (and others) pointing yet again to the close foreknowledge possessed by some *Searchlight*/state operatives in such matters, particularly those involved in the printing trade.

18 Footnote 26 page 11.

19 It's a great pity many on the Left don't think state agents/intervention in the Right are worthy of study — for instance even the landmark book by Tony Bunyan, *The Political Police in Britain* (Quartet 1977) contains no reference to state attitudes towards fascists in the 1970's, when these were undoubtedly rife, and important.

20 On this see Tom Metzger's *WAR — 'White Aryan Resistance'* August 1993, Editorial p.2/reproduction of what looks like a page from the *Los Angeles Times* p.8. The 'outing' of Allen seems to have been something of a coup for *genuine* 'Nazi Counter-Intelligence' (as opposed to the spurious 'Nazi Counter-Intelligence' *Searchlight* allege I'm a member of — see 'At War With Society' July 1993 p.18), although (understandably) that wasn't how this case was reported in the UK press . . .

21 See *At War With The Truth* (1993) p.9-10.

22 Because of persistent rumours that he has incited violence against me personally, claiming to be in possession of personal details about myself that were he not a *Searchlight*/state operative he wouldn't possess (whether accurate or not).

23 Plausible denial isn't helped by the fact that the only contact address on this magazine is Covington's.

24 *Evening Standard* 11/5/94.

25 Appendix 3 p.25-6.

26 *Einherjar* would not have been openly submitted in case at some future date the true identity of the authors became widely known, in which case they may hypothetically be charged with breaching parliamentary privilege.

27 On which, see Philip Willan's *Puppet Masters: the Political Use of Terrorism in Italy* (Constable 1991), reviewed by myself in *Lobster* 23 June 1992 p.28-30.

28 The NF today does very well in this regard, with very high 'production values' evident in their recent brochure *The National Front* (March 1994), although that might be related to the £120,000 bequest that came their way in 1994.

29 The physical confrontations in December, as a result of which both Eddy Butler and Tony Lecomber apparently came off worst will have stiffened Tyndall's resolve.

30 See Tyndall's 'A New Era For Nationalism' *Spearhead* January 1994 p.6-8 which argues the case for electoral advance.

31 See articles by Eddie Butler and Tony Lecomber in *Spearhead* July 1994 on this.

32 *The Order* issue 6 February 1994, Editorial.

33 *Evening Standard* 11/5/94 p19.

34 For the BNP view see *Spearhead* May 1994 p.19 and June 1994 p.3.

35 July/August 1994 issue p.12.

36 Press Statement p.2.

37 I am not issuing a futile call for 'pacifism' on the streets, merely suggesting that the

intervention of the state however helpful it may seem to be in the short term, is no substitute for the capabilities of a strong independent anti-fascist movement. Ironically, in recent years the amounts of papers sold every week by fascists has hovered around the 20-30 mark, well below what sales were in the 1970's (hundreds) reflecting a change in the social composition of the neighbourhood. By forcing the BNP to sell elsewhere, the authorities may well have done them a favour, although I don't suppose that was the intention. In any case, the importance of Brick Lane is symbolic, given that Mosley's BUF used to sell there in the 1930's.

38   Someone who fascists allege was murdered by the state.

39   On the costs of policing demonstrations, see *Police Review* 25/2/94 p.18-19, 'What Price Protest' (Claire Casey). On the events of 15/1, see 'Combat 18 — Back to Basics (Anti-Fascist Action), and 'Police Stop Gig for Ian' (*The Order* issue 6 February 1994)/*Putsch* 9 February 1994 p.5. *Target* 5 Spring 1994 p.4 contends that the source of AFA knowledge of the location was the police, not their own scouts. Although how fascists would know exactly what AFA scouts were up to that day isn't clear.

40   See *The Order* issue 5 'Beware the State is After You' (p.10-11) and also *Sigrun* (British Movement) issue 2 December 1993 p.2 for an impassioned statement of opposition to the "virtual police state we are now living in".

41   Gianfranco Sanguinetti *On Terrorism & the State* (London 1982) p.58.

42   See articles in the *Guardian* 13/4/94 and the *Jewish Chronicle* 22/4/94, this last one written by Home Office minister Peter Lloyd.

43   See pages xxvi-xxxvi.

The gallery enlarged — green targets enter the frame

THUS FAR, the target groups dealt with have all at some time featured in MI5's sights before — *Meibion Glyndwr* for example, were subject to such attention as far back as 1980.[1] What MI5 seems to have done with them is by means of entrapment, propaganda and so forth, upgraded the existing targets, as well as reoriented their relationship with each other. This in itself is disturbing enough, however current trends point to this only being the tip of the iceberg. Upgrading the activities of these groups alone is not enough to fill the gap left by the collapse of the Soviet Empire, and so the net has been cast yet wider. The possibility of a drastic decline in Irish-related work for MI5 on top of that puts them in a difficult position indeed.

Even before the recent IRA 'ceasefire', various sections of the Green movement had long been seen as suitable candidates for the type of antics outlined above. Steven Dorrill tells us vaguely that the "Animal Liberation movement has now been mentioned as a suitable target for MI5", but gives no further details.[2] Gary Murray points out that both Greenpeace and Friends of the Earth are infiltrated,[3] and both he and Dorril express concern about such things, Dorril pointing out "there is no clear definition of terrorism, which creates some confusion and potential for abuse".[4] It is in this area, the intersection between the old 'New Left' and Greens, that much of the action is. The traditional far Left, including extra-parliamentary Trotskyists, have in general been very demoralised by the collapse of the USSR, whatever they thought of it. In which case, as John Callaghan (Politics Professor) put it in the *Independent on Sunday* (2/5/93), "the only really interesting area is anarchism — the rise of Class War and the animal liberation groups and the New Age hippies. There are real numbers there".

To my mind, this would explain the attention the Animal Liberation movement has been receiving from the state in recent times, including the use of *agents provocateurs*, some disclosed, others yet to be. It also explains the related interest in those concerned with 'Earth Liberation', whether it be in the 'Earth Liberation Front' or the entirely separate 'Earth First'. Recent events have accelerated this MI5/Special Branch interest, and brought it more into public view, but it was certainly there before.

Making the earth move . . .

Starting with Earth matters, in a particularly nasty piece, on 15/10/92 the *Evening Standard* ran a feature investigating the growth of 'militant groups in the capital'. The author (or should I say 'conduit') Paul Charman wrote that "security experts are also concerned about the dramatic rise in the number of 'New Age' groups on the fringes of the Green movement who are prepared to use terror in support of animal rights and ecology issues". Earth First, an entirely peaceful group committed to 'non-violent direct action' in all circumstances, was described as an assemblage of outcast 'Greens', and he informed us that "some of the more extreme activists are thought to operate in 'underground' cells". The address and photograph of the then distribution-base for *Earth First Action Update* was printed, sandwiched between that for the neo-nazi Blood & Honour network and helpful advice from Charman to readers: "as well as expressing sympathy or support for terrorist activity, they are also potential targets for attacks from rival groups". This theme was returned to again in the *Evening Standard* (10/12/93), this time in an article by Tony Maguire, commenting on 'growing support' for ELF cells, and (in classic use of the 'interweaving' technique analysed above in relation to Scotland), merging consideration of the ELF, Earth First and an ethical shop-lifting outfit CRISP. The utter devastation already wrought upon Twyford Down by the incessant road-building programme, and the damage being done elsewhere, in the undisclosed attempt to build a whole new network of motorways to lead from the Channel Tunnel to the whole country, means anti-roads protestors aren't going to go away. Hitherto, the state has made heavy use of private security firms (such as Brays Detective Agency & Group 4) for surveillance and other purposes.[5] The increasing self-awareness of some protestors has led to a burgeoning political consciousness which quite rightly worries the state, and the road-builders.[6] An especially interesting development has been the anonymous publication of the *Terra-ist* magazine, only one issue so far (Spring 1994). The editorial sharply differentiates the magazine from Earth First, placing the publication firmly in sympathy with the ELF, an organisation born in the aftermath of the Twyford Down protest. The *Terra-ist* is well aware of the need for proper security, something lost on many in the Green movement, rightly criticising Earth First UK for listing home addresses as contact points: the article by Charman mentioned above shows the danger of that. Sympathy for the street tactics of Anti-Fascist Action are openly expressed, and all in all this strand of consciousness is a quantum leap in terms of the Green movement. Similarly, a leaflet anonymously distributed to advertise the occasional 'Earth Nights', whereby the ELF asks supporters to inflict economic sabotage against the "forces of reaction" is equally interested in a wide front of struggle, calling for "a broad alliance of environmental, animal liberation, worker, anti-fascist and revolutionary groups".

This then is the back-ground, and state assets have been busy bees indeed, attempting to crush, distort and manipulate such initiatives. The most simple form this has taken is the spreading of lies and general disinformation about the tactics of the anti-road lobby. Following on from a fairy-story in *Construction News* (30/6/94) falsely alleging 'man-traps' had been set by anti-road protestors, John Harlow wrote a much-criticised article in the *Sunday Times* entitled 'Green Guerillas booby-trap sites' (3/7/94). This sought to transfer the blame for violence at road-sites onto the victims, and contained specious attacks on the ELF, quoting a Group 4 operative as describing "strong links between urban anarchists such as Class War & the ELF". The article brought about a furious response from anti-roads groups.[7]

Propaganda is one thing though, and by no means the primary route for state intervention. They are particularly interested in placing agents inside groups, and setting them up where they don't exist. Until recently, before the ELF Prisoner's Support network was set up, there was a 'window of opportunity' for state assets. What I am referring to is the fact that while the ELF is, like the ALF, a militant underground body using a cell structure, unlike the ALF it has no recognised official (but non-operational) spokesperson, in the way the ALF has for instance, in Robin Webb, who though not connected with illegal activity in any way can nevertheless knowledgeably comment on and speculate about any animal rights actions that are carried out. The animal rights movement also has those two excellent publications, the *ALF Support Group Newsletter* and *Arkangel*, as well as *Turning Point* and a host of other smaller magazines. ELF actions are covered elsewhere, especially in *Green Anarchist*, but there has not been a tangible support structure.

It is into *this* breach that state agents have sought to enter. The first of note, Tim Hepple, I have already written about elsewhere (in *At War With The Truth*), and I merely refer readers to that publication, especially pages 10-11. I can now though, for the first time, alert readers to another fascist, this time with no apparent connections to *Searchlight*, but whose actions and agenda seem to be very close to MI5's, and whose trajectory and methodology, inciting violence and causing disruption wherever he goes, especially in the animal rights movement, seem to parallel almost exactly that of Hepple. Much more will be said of this person, Stuart McCullough of the International Third Position, elsewhere, but one thing can be revealed now. Running back to his now-defunct Belfast PO Box, Stuart McCullough and others, actually *set up* a dummy ELF mailing address, BM ELF, London WC1N 3XX. This, the ELF, is an organisation (and a cause) McCullough had previously never shown any interest in at all, and the setting up of a dummy group would seem to perfectly fit the 'pseudo-gang' model. How fascinating that when virtually no fascists have ever even heard of the ELF, he should seek to set one up, even going to the extent of producing bogus (and not entirely convincing) leaflets. I can assure McCullough and those behind him that the proof I have is irrefutable, so challenge me if you dare![8] The targetting of an individual alleged to be behind the distribution address for *Terra-ist*, also engaged in by John Harlow in the *Sunday Times* (11/9/94), in which article Harlow openly admits receiving information from Special Branch, is also noteworthy.

Even if the ELF now has a prisoner support structure, its necessarily ethereal nature means that all sorts of lies, fitting in with state agendae, are being disseminated about it. A particularly outrageous one, but wholly logical, is the story that another Special Branch journalistic asset suggested recently to the homeless magazine the *Big Issue* that they cover. This was one concerning the links between ecotage (ecological sabotage) and *Combat 18!* The creation of fictitious and mendacious links such as these fits in with MI5's *and* Special Branches agenda. In order to cover up for their assets, confuse the political scene, encourage conflict, and carry out actions themselves, undetected, MI5 and Special Branch need to create as much complexity, confusion and disinformation as possible, using assets in the media and on the ground, as well as under it.

Events in the USA, where entrapment and framing of Earth First activists is rife, show just how dangerous the secret state can be in this area, one the FBI seems to have pioneeered. The case study in *Covert Action Quarterly*, covering the operation against Judi Bari, which went so far as planting a bomb in her car that injured her, and then charging her and the other occupant with 'illegal possession of explosives', shows the depths these people will sink to.[9] The fact that the agency involved is the FBI, seeking to extend its tentacles into Europe, whether it be 'investigating' nazis, organised crime or whatever, and thereby making alliances with the likes of MI5, is cause for alarm indeed. It is my view that Hepple (and McCullough), as well as others we are not yet aware of, were directed to take an interest in the Green movement in order to produce scenarios similar to the one affecting Judi Bari.

Setting the animals free?

State interest in the area of Animal Liberation, whether it be the ALF, the recently-revived Hunt Retribution Squad, the Justice Department or the Animal Rights Militia, is long-standing. Speaking as a close observer, at present I see no indications that those groups are doing anything other than they claim to be: ie if they are infiltrated, it isn't readily evident. They are carrying out actions conforming to their own logic and agendas, just like the ELF seem to have been. Thus they are not, in any sense, 'pseudo-gangs'. However, just as with C18, the state is desperately *seeking* to influence them, to put their assets 'in place', and distort their functioning. The animal rights movement is very resilient, and has proved itself a tough nut to crack so far. Indeed, irrespective of the specific details, the quality of the various documents produced in recent years, such as *Into the 90's with the ALF, Interviews With ALF Activists*, and the most recent *Going Underground,* makes them stand out as classics of underground political literature.[10] There have been attempts to suborn the animal liberation movement, and some of these I will analyse at greater length elsewhere: I am thinking particularly of events in Bristol 1989-90, when various actions attributed to animal activists have the hallmark of the state. One thing that must (and does) worry those in the state who seek to intervene is the fact that the animal rights movement can on occasions fight back on the legal terrain, and win spectacular victories, as in Hudders-field December 1992.[11]

Major attempts have been made to portray the ALF (which has an unwavering commitment to non-violence) and similar bodies as 'terrorist', with even the likes of Richard Clutterbuck getting in on the act.[12] An article in *Police Review* by Mark Matfield (Research Defence Society) said that "in mainland Britain, the ALF is the most active terrorist group",[13] and while he may be said to have a direct self-interest in saying this, others too have echoed the sentiments, and more recently. In the *Sunday Times* for 28/8/94, David Leppard, who writes extensively on Northern Ireland/MI5, but not to my knowledge on Green matters, penned a lurid and highly significant article, under the headline 'Animal Rights Activists turn to IRA tactics'. After outlining various actions carried out by the Justice Department (not of course Welling), he went on to say that Scotland Yard have become involved "after intelligence leaks from informers inside the animal rights movement that the extremists have decided to target people rather than property". He then went on to retail what is the classic indication of state *agent provocateur* interest in any group: "Scotland Yard has discovered that animal rights extremists are trying to buy plastic explosives on the black market. They have also infiltrated the Territorial Army to obtain weapons and explosives". Given this is *not* based in fact (where are the names of people charged?), it is a statement of intent: on behalf of both Special Branch and Leppard's more usual sources, MI5. This article, days before the IRA ceasefire was announced, had the following chilling message, that "senior Special Branch detectives say the group poses the biggest single threat to security on the mainland after the IRA". Now of course, the Justice Department, only in existence a few months, finds itself at the top of the list. Other articles on MI5's role post-ceasefire also made mention of animal rights activists.[14]

I have already drawn attention to the contrast between the ELF and ALF: that the latter has a visible and highly respected spokesperson Robin Webb, who also performs the public service of commenting on Justice Department and other similar actions. If elements of the secret state are going to effectively disrupt the animal liberation movement, then removing ready access to an articulate spokesperson would be very clever indeed, as a preparatory measure. Now there is a cogent reasoned argument for doing away with the ALF Press Officer and indeed the name ALF, for reasons that I fully understand. These arguments are well put in *Going Underground . . . For Animal Liberation* (anonymous December 1993). However, on balance, speaking as an outsider, I think the ALF would be well advised to keep the structure as it is: but obviously that's a matter for them, not me.[15] Anyway, the most salient opinion here is at present, I would suggest, the state's.

In recent times, action has already been set in train to try and 'take out' Robin Webb as Press Officer, fully consistent with the violent agenda of Special Branch (and MI5). On 5/9/94, in Brighton, as he left a private house, six carloads of police, including members of Scotland Yard's 'Anti-Terrorist Squad' (SO13) pounced on him.

They immediately strode to the boot of his car (as if they already knew where to look) and triumphantly flourished a sawn-off shotgun that they had 'found' there. Their contention was that they were acting on a 'tip-off'. Robin Webb was charged with possession of such, and much to their annoyance, remained free, on bail. This affair reeks of a set-up: not only would Robin Webb be the last person in the world to use violence against a person, or any living creature, the whole arrest was suspicious. If it was believed he knew there was a shot-gun in his car, why were the officers not armed as they approached? Also, if someone was stupid enough to carry round a shotgun, then mightn't they keep this in the front of a car, under a blanket? How did the police know it was there? A rhetorical question, given they almost certainly planted it. The choice of weapon too is strange, one that has no conceivable defensive use, rather more suitable for mass indiscriminate violence. Not something Webb or the ALF have ever been into, but fitting the image which the state and animal abusers would like to convey about animal rights activists. The idea would be/is to remove him, or at least discredit him, so that 'rogue units' and 'pseudo gangs' can then enter onto the scene. If Scotland Yard have information on 'plastics explosives' purchases then it is most likely because it is they who have been seeking to procure such, perhaps they might care to investigate their own ranks? I do hope that wasn't where all the missing money recently stolen by the Metropolitan Police's chief accountant went: perish the thought.

Historically, even before the setting up of ARNI (Animal Rights National Index) at Scotland Yard in 1984, investigation of animal activists has been the province of Special Branch. The intriguing careers of both Hepple and McCullough though, do not seem to fit into an SB pattern, far too grandiose and wide-ranging for that. In which case, we could be seeing a new inter-agency conflict looming. By expanding its interest in militant sections of the Green movement, MI5 may be entering into a new phase of the 'turf war' with Special Branch, which neither can afford to lose. Each will vie with the other to run *agents provocateurs* and set up activists, in a vicious spiral as a result of which all things Green will definitely be the loser. In this, as in other areas, I am *not* saying the impetus is necessarily coming from the government: so when the Home Office Minister of State, Lord Ferrers, said that he disagreed with 'anti-terror laws' against animal rights extremists, because it would be going too far "to equate that with terrorism",[16] I don't disbelieve him. What I am saying is that here, as in other areas, it is in the interests of fractions of the state apparatus to make such assertions/connections. What they then seek to do is create a situation whereby the government will feel it has to respond in the way they (MI5/Special Branch) would like it to, while not being aware they are being manipulated. At other times it's not like that, the government instigates or enthusiastically colludes with illegality: I'm just saying it varies.

A sociological digression

The big political issue of 1994 for many has been the 'Criminal Justice Bill', about to go through its final parliamentary stages having failed to clear all the hurdles in the summer. As many have remarked (though not the Labour party leadership), this is a truly frightening piece of legislation. I do not intend to repeat all the excellent points made elsewhere by others.[17] The point that interests me though, is that many of those whose activities will be made illegal: squatters, hunt saboteurs, travellers, young people attending 'raves', and political demonstrators generally (including Welsh language activists, for whom civil disobedience is a crucial tactic) are exactly the sorts of people who may well have an interest in animal rights and anti-road activities. What is being created, in effect, is a sociological 'outgroup' who will find, at a stroke, many of the liberties they have taken for granted will just not be there any more. This (deliberate creation of outlaws) was not the conscious intention behind the legislation, but that will be its partial effect. Other groups have been 'floated' as possible targets in unrelated developments. Most notably, the Hell's Angels motorcycling fraternity, who in May 1993 were accused at a conference of the (rival to MI5) 'National Crime Intelligence Service' of "being responsible for more assaults and murders than any other organised gang in Britain, and of being the fastest growing criminal outfit in the world"[18]

The marginalisation of some groups and the inclusion of others is another form of 'divide and rule', integral to the state's manipulation of dissent, so the reported remarks to a recent conference of Chief Constables by *Liberty* General Secretary Andrew Puddephatt seem unfortunate. He is described as having urged them to talk to the (anti-CJB) "Freedom Network about drawing up codes of conduct over how the public order sections of the bill are implemented"[19] This is creating a distinction between 'legitimate dissent' and that which isn't, and the shadowy 'Interactive Diners Club', reportedly an Oxbridge coterie, don't strike me as being persons whose political judgement should be the ultimate arbiter of anything. I can well understand them having little time for the 'parachute politics' of the SWP, who have jumped into the issue for recruitment purposes (making the CJB the focus of this year's 'College Recruitment Demonstration' at the start of October). However, rumoured opposition to the SWP on the grounds they are too *radical* and might call some sort of *Intifada* in opposition to the CJB, is way off beam. The problem with the SWP isn't that they might take the fight against the CJB to such lengths: the difficulty is that they are just liberal *Guardian*-readers with placards (and lollipops) who take virtually no issue consistently seriously *enough*, except recruitment to their own party, to which anything and everything (including internal democracy and real political debate) have long been sacrificed.

Returning to the CJB, it will have sociological effects of use to MI5, by creating large numbers of disempowered, angry and also apathetic people, who sometimes will have an interest in exactly the types of 'new politics' represented by the Green-Left axis, particularly anarchists, eco-activists and animal liberationists. But MI5 weren't responsible for those parts of the bill, in this case the responsibility must lie more with the political classes, both the Tories for proposing it, and the craven Blair-led Labour Party for acquiescing in it.

The big picture

Here we have a situation where MI5 is in severe identity crisis, seeking to expand its empire in order to survive. They push for control of mainland anti-IRA/Loyalist operations, but realise that that on its own is hardly likely to yield the level of 'terrorist threat' necessary to maintain and expand their budgets, as well as, crucially, keep in employment valuable specialists in the area of 'domestic subversion', whether Left Right or Green. It is certainly not beyond the bounds of possibility that elements in MI5, in order to retain said experts, go about creating the very 'links' necessary to justify this. It wouldn't be a question of plucking such links entirely from thin air — the sympathies of Red Action and fascists towards different paramilitary organisations in Northern Ireland are well known. There is a world of difference though between a general affinity, up to and including propaganda distribution, and *operational* links, and it is these that MI5 may well have set about manufacturing. I say this not because I accept for one minute the guilt of any of those charged, but as a general hypothesis, based on knowledge in the public domain. In this volatile atmosphere, the activities outlined in *A Lie Too Far* (and the sequel *At War With the Truth*) do fit — the passing of disinformation, seeking to escalate political violence, suspicious fore-knowledge by a (self-confessed) state operative of the contents of Right-wing hitlists and so on. The intent would be to drive sections of the Green movement, anarchists, anti-fascists *and* fascists in a 'terrorist' direction, thus giving the spectre of 'domestic terrorism' a tangible form. The targetting of anarchist bookshops for attack by fascists in recent times may well have occurred not just because of reasons internal to fascist logic, but because MI5 assets placed in the far right might well have been 'activated' to encourage such attacks. It is speculation certainly, but these are troubling questions, and the similarity/chronological closeness of what seems to have been provocative state actions concerning far Left *and* far Right points towards the secret state — MI5. All this is hardly on the grand scale of the 'Wilson Plot', and while a minimum political agenda is MI5 retaining jobs and prestige, the overall agenda has yet to be ascertained. For instance, the European aspect is an intriguing one, and there have been disturbing parallels in terms of shadowy and violent 'pseudo-groups' in the Netherlands, and there is a very suspicious set of circumstances in Sweden also. Additionally, a moot question that arises must be one concerning whether the new turn in MI5 strategy was an *operational* one, involving giving the nod to selected personnel in autonomous units alone, or a *policy* one, disseminated more widely. I tend to the former option as being more likely, not only because it would thereby be far easier to keep the lid on it, but also because Stella Rimington's earlier experience in 'F' Branch will have laid the groundwork for a covert 'chain of command' leading down to those engaging at will in illegal actions. Tawdry as such activities are, they have had very real financial, and more importantly human, costs. It is unfortunately very likely that Special Branch agents will soon be engaging in very similar *agent provocateur* activities themselves.

Some of the above is conjecture, and guarded at that, but hopefully has provided an adequate framework within which to properly evaluate the bland words of *MI5 — The Security Service*. The message is loud and clear — 'business as usual for the secret state'. For the above insights into current MI5 methods — eavesdropping in a big way, bribery, *agents provocateurs*, supplying explosives/arms, mass surveillance, planting evidence, placing people on hit lists, engaging in trial by media and so on — are mainly derived from events *on the mainland*. What MI5 are getting up to in Ulster itself is most probably even more horrific . . .

Notes:

1 (London) *City Limits* 12/2/82 reported MI5 bugging a North Wales public telephone box that January (p.30).

2 *Silent Conspiracy* 1993 p.248.

3 *Enemies of the State* 1993 p.292-3.

4 *Op. cit.* p.248.

5 See for example *Daily Telegraph* 27/2/93.

6 See 'To be or not to be paranoid' by Annette Tibbles in *Do Or Die* 1994 p.43-44 for an example of increasing awareness of security matters.

7 See Lancashire Earth First! Press Release 11/7/94, letter from Tania de St Croix (Solsbury Hill Campaign) 6/7/94, and *Sunday Times* letters page 10/7/94. Maybe, given the amount of public support they have, Earth First & so on will get somewhere with the Press Complaints Commission: my personal experience of the Commission leads me to see it as an organisation that is beneath even contempt.

8 His career will be dealt with in full and gory detail in a forthcoming publication. Obviously, I will, as I did with Hepple before him, give him a full opprtunity to explain his actions, and should he (or any other state asset) want to come clean about his exploits, then all well and good. I am not interested in 'persecuting' individual agents, rather I hope to help them see the error of their ways, and put right any damage they may have caused.

9 Issue 47 Winter 1993-4 p.4-9/54-59.

10 Which makes politically illiterate and stupid comments from tedious Trotskyists, like the correspondent in *Workers Power* September 1994, Colin Lloyd, who described the ALF as Tories, laughable, to say the least.

11 On this see *Huddersfield 4 The State 0*, an account of the trial and ultimate acquittal of people accused of being ALF 'members'.

12 See *Black Flag* 166 25/1/87 p.2.

13 26/11/93 p.20.

14 See eg Richard Norton Taylor in the *Guardian* 1/9/94 and Julian Kossoff/Tony Thompson *Time Out* 7/9/94 p.13.

15 The ongoing debate is covered in *As Long As There Are Slaughterhouses There will be battlefields* (1991), and *SARP Newsletter* September-October 1992, April & May 1993.

16 *Guardian* 22/2/94.

17 For example, Liberty's *Briefing* of January 1994, and see also their *Agenda* magazine June 1994 p.8-9.

18 *Daily Telegraph* 29/5/93.

19 *Guardian* 6/8/94.